# Ecological Ethics: An Introduction

## Patrick Curry

polity

The right of Patrick Curry to be identified as Author of this Work has been asserted
in accordance with the UK Copyright, Designs and Patents Act 1988.

First published in 2006 by Polity Press

Polity Press
65 Bridge Street
Cambridge CB2 1UR, UK.

Polity Press
350 Main Street
Malden, MA 02148, USA

ISBN: 0-7456-2907-5
ISBN: 0-7456-2908-3 (pb)

A catalogue record for this book is available from the British Library.

Typeset in 11 on 13pt Bembo
by Servis Filmsetting Ltd, Manchester
Printed and bound in Great Britain by T.J. International Ltd, Padstow, Cornwall

The publisher has used its best endeavours to ensure that the URLs for external
websites referred to in this book are correct and active at the time of going to press.
However, the publisher has no responsibility for the websites and can make no
guarantee that a site will remain live or that the content is or will remain appropriate.

Every effort has been made to trace all copyright holders, but if any have been
inadvertently overlooked the publishers will be pleased to include any necessary
credits in any subsequent reprint or edition.

For further information on Polity, visit our website: www.polity.co.uk

Printed on FSC certified paper.

# Contents

# Acknowledgements

This book began life six years ago as a short essay for the website of ECO, a British online group which flew the flag for ecocentrism as long as personal resources permitted, so I would like to thank warmly Sue Birley, Val Stevens, Harry Cripps, Barbara Droop and (somewhat more peripherally) Sandy Irvine for their interest.

For their helpful comments on earlier drafts, I am very grateful to Nigel Cooper, David Orton, Michael and Penny Novack, Ariel Salleh, Val Stevens and the late Stan Rowe. Harry Cripps, Clay Ramsay and (as ever) Michael Winship also made valuable suggestions for some chapters.

I would also like to acknowledge the moral and intellectual support of the members of Left Bio, the online discussion group whose ethos is integral to the spirit of this book and several of whose names appear elsewhere in these acknowledgements.

I am very much beholden to John B. Thompson, Andrea Drugan and Sarah Dancy of Polity Press, who made this book possible and with whom it has been a pleasure to work.

Among my other personal debts, for putting up with a father sometimes doubling as a writer I would like to thank my daughter Sylva, and her mother Suzanna; my own late mother, Noreen Curry, who loved wild places and animals and introduced me to many; for walking the talk, Anne Carpenter, Vincent Chambers, Jo Dubiel, Tom Martin, Yannis Mitzelos, Tim Robinson, John Sleep and Tim Winship; in addition to most of the above people, other friends who have encouraged my writing: David Abram, Laurence Coupe, Stephen Fitzpatrick, Patrick Joyce, Sean Kane, Ray Keenoy, Brian Kennedy, Kigen-san Licha, Tom Martin, Garey Mills, Yannis Mitzelos, Susan Peters, Neil Platts, Martine Sandor and Joanna Savory; for their hospitality at a key point in my getting to grips with the manuscript, Howard and Annette Preston; for their personal and practical support, my sister Kathy and, notwithstanding any differences of opinion, my brothers Mark and Steele; for helping to keep the bodily show on the road, my teacher and friend Dwyer Evelyn of Physical Arts; and for direct experience of an ethic of care arising from reverence for life, the late Kobun Chino Otagawa, his dharma heir Vanja Palmers, Pepi Stuegger and members of the sangha whose spiritual home is Puregg. Finally, I want to thank all the green places and non-human persons who have so enriched my life, and to whom I hope hereby to give a little back.

This book is dedicated to the unsung activists struggling – against the odds and always at the cost of an easy life – to protect the natural world we all share from its many enemies. They are not thereby misanthropes but (as the late Stan Rowe once described himself) defenders of the Earth against the excesses of anthropes: Earthlings worthy of the name.

The author can be contacted at <ee@gn.apc.org>

# 1

## Introduction

## This Book

This book is intended to do what the title says: introduce readers, clearly and critically, to the subject as a whole. It is not meant to provide an in-depth analysis of any one school or thinker, nor will it try to arrive at philosophical conclusions that are irrefutable. It seeks only to refresh and enlarge the current cultural conversation, in the broadest sense, with some timely ideas and values. In particular, my goal is to suggest a promising and reasonably coherent set of ethical principles, based on ecocentric values, which could make a significant positive contribution to life – including, but not only, our life – on Earth.

The subject is *ethics*, or, put at its simplest, the question of how one should live and act. In particular, it is a relatively new subject called *ecological ethics*. In this view, ethical questions can no longer be restricted to how to treat other human beings, or even animals, but must embrace the entire natural world.

In the context of the 'Western' philosophical tradition, this is a very recent suggestion indeed. (The idea itself is not new, but the idea of taking it seriously is.) It has only come to the fore in the past thirty years, in exact parallel with increasing awareness of the worsening global ecological crisis. And that crisis is the ultimate context for this book. My hope and intention is for it to make a positive difference, however small, not only in university departments but outside them, in the wider world.

Of course, enough time has passed for several good textbooks on the subject to appear.[1] What is distinctive about this one, however, is its acceptance of specifically ecological ethics, in the fullest and deepest sense. Unlike, it seems, most other authors, I take the view that there is nothing inherently difficult, obscure or problematic about doing so, requiring extra caution when venturing forth from the human stockade. Similarly, there are many other books which address standard ethical concepts; so although I do too, I spend longer on the relatively neglected ethics of Deep Ecology, Gaia Theory, ecofeminism and so on.

This book therefore doesn't advocate ethics by 'extension' from human beings through other animals (mostly those lucky enough to resemble people in some way that is valued) to, perhaps, and only after much agonizing, trees.[2] Rather, I *start* from the belief, or perception, that nature – which certainly includes humanity – is the ultimate source of all value. And simply put, what is valued is what ultimately determines ethics. People will not treat properly whoever or whatever they do not care about. So, as Richard Sylvan and David Bennett put it, 'the ecological community forms the ethical community' (1994: 91).

Does this seem far-fetched? Perhaps, in the sense of being currently unusual, but as the same authors point out: 'Part of the task of implementing environmental ethics consists in imagining and aiming for what lies entirely beyond the bounds of present practice, thinking the unthinkable' (ibid. 182). We could also consider this: is not everything humanity has ever done, in the broadest possible sense, a development, no matter how refined, of the Earth out of which we have evolved, and of which we are still composed? More: take away the Earth and its so-called support-systems, and all life-forms, including you and me, would vanish without a trace. Is it then something of which we need take no heed? Looked at in this way, an ecological ethic surely amounts to profound common sense.

But it is also an important part of this book to argue that even enlightened self-interest is not enough, in at least two ways. One is that the non-human nature with which we share the Earth deserves as serious moral consideration as do humans. The other is that unless nature gets such consideration, its richest and most wonderful places and the greater part of our fellow Earthlings are unlikely, as a direct result of our self-centredness, to survive this century; and that will be at least as great a crime as any we have committed against each other.

Furthermore, notwithstanding our usual intense entanglements with ourselves and those in our immediate circle, even modern human beings have not entirely lost touch with an awareness of our profound involvement in, and dependence on, the natural world. Many people, perhaps (for some) a surprising number, still 'feel they live within a vast whole – nature – which is in some sense the source of all value, and whose workings are quite generally entitled to respect' (Midgley 1997: 95–6). This is surely a sign of hope.

## Value and Nature

As we shall see, there is a spectrum of perceived value proceeding from that which is entirely restricted to humanity, which can be called **anthropocentric** (meaning human-centred), through to thoroughly **ecocentric** (Earth-centred). It follows, then, that I shall be concentrating increasingly on the latter as we proceed through that spectrum, looking at the strengths of each major position on it, but also limitations that point to the need for a more ecocentric alternative. However, I would like to make it clear that ecological ethics is not intended to *replace* traditional human-centred ethics – which has a perfectly legitimate and important role in intra-human relationships – or its extensions to, say, animals. The point is rather, by adding something new, to enable ethical behaviour which anthropocentric ethics cannot. (I would add that once we arrive at a fully deep or dark green ethic, there will also be no attempt to judge between the several different kinds which is the 'most ecocentric'; here too, each has its strengths and weaknesses.)

The same reasoning explains why I have not called the subject, as it is more commonly known, 'environmental ethics'.[3] While there is no point in trying to ban the term, 'environment' is widely understood in its literal meaning, namely that which surrounds. It thus denotes a passive setting which is really of secondary interest to the stars: us. In recent years, the term has acquired a more abstract and scientific dimension, designating the biological processes and systems that sustain — once again, so far as most people are concerned — us.[4] But in either case, the term lends itself far too readily to two assumptions that contribute massively to ecological crisis: (1) that ultimately, only 'we' matter (which, in practice, is usually restricted to only some humans at that); and (2) that the value, and indeed reality, of everything else need only concern us to the extent that it enables us to get on with our own show.

To be sure, 'ecological' is not without its difficulties too. The word was coined in 1866 by the German natural philosopher Ernst Haeckel, who borrowed the Greek word *oikos*, meaning 'home' or 'household', to describe the scientific study of the relationships among organisms and between them and their environments. In recent years, however, it has acquired a more general popular meaning that is sometimes seriously at odds with its original one — personally and/or politically engaged, for example, where the scientific version is apparently detached. Furthermore, almost any subject or its study which emphasizes interrelationships is now often described as (for example) the ecology of cities, or family ecology, etc.

In this way a whole range of meanings has now evolved, and confusion can arise if the kind of ecology intended is not made clear. But there is no reason to allow biologists proprietary rights over 'ecology'. For our purposes, 'ecological' is now also commonly understood, quite legitimately, to describe a metaphysical and/or political philosophy centred on nature.

## Ethics and Grub

It might be asked, why do we need ethics at all and thus, by implication, a book such as this? We shall look more closely at the nature of ethics in chapter 3, but nothing there will take away from the meanings that any reader probably already brings to it: questions like, What is good? And what (if anything) is the ultimate good? What is the best way to live? Or the right way to be, or at least to act? Of course, these can be very troubling questions, and for many people, both as individuals and collectively, in any kind of organization, it is often easier to avoid them. This has led to the convenient assumption (for some) that ethics is, at best, some kind of special subject which is separate from, and therefore ultimately an optional add-on to, the rest of life. To put it crudely, as did Bertold Brecht, 'Grub first, then ethics.' But this too is a statement of a particular kind of ethics, not an absence of it! And once having adopted such a view, grub is usually followed by a long list of other concerns which apparently also take precedence over ethics. When these extend to personal security, comfort and glamour, a single person purchasing a four-wheel SUV for use in the city, for example, can seem to make perfect sense.

The view of ethics as optional is not only nonsense – as if anyone lived or acted without any idea of what is good, and therefore right (however perverted from another ethical point of view) – but dangerous nonsense, because the consequences affect us all. And when I say 'all', I don't just mean human beings. With the possible exception of those living in extreme poverty where simple physical survival is an issue, there are always choices available regarding how to acquire one's grub, to say nothing of other goods, and some will be distinctly more ethically defensible than others. To pretend otherwise simply allows the values that *do* guide our choices to go unexamined and undiscussed, often under a cloak of a 'sensible consensus'.

Lately, when pressed, some committees have taken to hiring an 'ethicist'. But ethics, properly understood, is a dimension of *every* human experience and enterprise; it cannot safely be left to others to take care of. As Joseph R. Des Jardins puts it, 'Leaving environmental decisions to the "experts" in science and technology does not mean that these decisions will be objective and value neutral. It means only that the values and philosophical assumptions that do decide the issue will be those that these experts hold' (2001: 7).

This point applies just as much to ecology as to any other field. The human-driven processes causing the present destruction of the natural world – unprecedented, if not in scale, in being the result of the activities of a single species – are not unethical in the sense that ethics is missing. On the contrary, they are saturated with a particular kind of ethics which happens to be ecologically pathological, but which doesn't get much talked or thought about. At that point, as someone once remarked, 'we do not have the idea; it has us' (quoted in Wenz 2000: 238). So ethics matters, ecological ethics in particular, and it is urgently important to raise its public profile.

A related point is that ethics is not, and never can be, like mathematics or the so-called exact sciences. That is, ethics cannot provide a watertight set of rules to be applied mechanically, that will save anyone the time and trouble of some hard thinking, and feeling, when confronted with a real, and therefore specific and unique, situation that presents an ethical dilemma. As we shall see, there is not necessarily always just one right thing to do. Life is complicated, and values can and do conflict. Whether personally or socially, ethics grows out of the ongoing interaction between one's ideas and values and the world, each affecting the other; and that doesn't happen without you, so to speak, being there.

## What's New?

Is an ecological ethic something new? Richard Routley first suggested in 1973 that there was now a need for 'a new, an environmental, ethic'. (Writing later as Richard Sylvan, he has been one of the principal influences on this book.) His suggestion led to a flurry of rearguard action by philosophers on behalf of the status quo. It was led by a fellow Australian, the late John Passmore, who maintained that what was needed was 'not so much a "new ethic" as a more general adherence to a perfectly familiar ethic' (1974: 186). According to that ethic, we are responsible only to fellow human beings; thus, it could include responsibilities *for* nature, insofar as that affects us, but not *to* nature.

Passmore's further point that 'A new ethic will arise out of existing attitudes, or not at all' (ibid. 56) is well taken, but it doesn't follow that another ethic – in its composition and intention, new – is impossible. 'New' always means relatively new. And I would add that in this instance, there is something ancient about an ecological ethic; it is something we have forgotten, rather than never known. Indeed, its fundamental intuition concerning the Earth and our fellow-creatures therein is still clear in the culture of virtually every indigenous people, where they have not been colonized by modern commerce (or simply exterminated). An awareness of the intimate relatedness and co-dependency of humans with plants, other animals and the places of the Earth still exists, I suggest, in our collective cultural memory. Deep Ecologists Bill Devall and George Sessions are right: the change that is needed involves a 'reawakening of something very old' (1985: ix).

As to whether such a 'new' ethic is *needed*, surely the answer is 'yes', and now more then ever. The continuing conservatism of philosophers (which is evident even in textbooks of environmental ethics) begs the question: if the ethics we already have is indeed adequate, why are we in such an ongoing, and worsening, mess? Presumably they would reject one possible answer, as I would, which is that ethics as such has no impact on what happens in the world. That would seem to leave the strong possibility, at least, that what we have (and may have been good enough in its time) is no longer up to the job.

In any case, the current human impact on nature is driven by institutionalized ideas and values which embody a very familiar ethic indeed, according to which the consequences of this impact simply do not matter. So a new ecological ethic is not only possible, but urgently needed. And as Sylvan and Bennett say, 'Changing to respectful approaches to the environment and supplanting the place of humans in the world and their ethical systems may seem excessive and extreme. Yet what is now seen as unthinkable, as the voice of extremism, will in a decade or two be seen as necessity' (1994: 184).

# Transparency

Finally, I make every effort to be comprehensive, fair and even-handedly critical within the ambit of the subject. However, let me point out that the author of every book, without exception, also takes positions; but in keeping with certain academic conventions, they are usually relatively covert – and therefore, ironically, harder to perceive, analyse and discuss.

The same point can be understood another way. We are used to a firm distinction between description (of what 'is') and prescription (of what we should do); the latter kind of statement is also called *normative*. But that distinction is founded more on intellectual habit than anything else. A particular description is only one way out of a theoretically unlimited number of ways the world, or any part thereof, could be described; it therefore also *prescribes* a particular way of looking at it. Equally, a normative or prescriptive statement also involves a particular description of the world, i.e., an assertion that it is one way and not another. It follows, then, that there is no point in pretending that it is possible to describe anything in a completely neutral or detached way. That still leaves the attempt at fairness, comprehensiveness and so on as an ideal that can, in certain situations, be healthy and helpful; but it must not be confused with the actuality, or even an ultimate ideal. We are all, intellectuals included, participating *in* the world, even when we are commenting *on* it. Observation is a kind of intervention, and vice versa. To pretend otherwise simply amounts to trying to avoid acknowledging and taking responsibility for one's own perspective.[5]

For this reason, I have decided to make my own assumptions, values and priorities explicit. Thus, something else that distinguishes this guide to ecological ethics from others is the fact that, ultimately, it is (openly) committed to a global ecological ethic and, by extension, to its realization in practice. That means its treatment of properly ecological ethics is, I believe, more thorough than those of any other textbooks. By the same token, I hope it will be of interest, use and maybe even inspiration not only to fellow members of the academy, whether teachers or students, but also to activists (who may be the same people, but often are not).

# 2

## The Earth in Crisis

### The Signs

This is not the place to spell out the current ecocrisis or its context in detail,[1] but since it is a primary reason why an ecological ethic is needed it must at least be pointed out. Of course, the human propensity for denial should never be underestimated. In the ecological field, it even has a high end in the form of well-publicized commentators reassuring us that, overall, everything is fine, even getting better.[2] Given the preponderance of otherwise bad news, these individuals have received media attention out of all proportion to their merit. But the remarkable thing about the global ecological crisis is that even though most analysts say it is serious, it really *is* serious – and getting worse. This is true on any major kind of indicator,[3] such as the following.

### Climate change

The overwhelming scientific consensus is that so-called global warming – almost certainly (i.e., with as much certainty as the subject permits) largely as a direct result of human overproduction of $CO^2$ – is now well under way.[4] Carbon dioxide levels are now the highest they have been for at least 440,000 years, and the effects may already be entering a stage of runaway positive feedback, worsening still further even if the Kyoto Accord was adhered to by all the major producers of greenhouse gases, and indeed strengthened. Yet that prospect currently seems unlikely, especially in the case of the country that is the greatest single source of greenhouse gases, the USA.[5] So despite the probable consequences of extreme weather conditions for all forms of life on the planet, ranging from stress to disaster, this enormous and wildly irresponsible experiment on our common and only home continues. As Madeleine Bunting writes: 'With a kind of savage justice, climate change is an issue which exposes the weakest link in the cultural mindset of Western market capitalism: the collective capacity for self-restraint in pursuit of a common good.'[6]

## Pollution

In addition to pollution driving climate change, tens of thousands of synthetic chemicals – potentially, at the very least, toxic: most are untested – have now been introduced into the environment, especially in the overdeveloped world. (Industrial dumping, however, favours the less developed world, where controls are laxer and an official blind eye is often easier, or at least cheaper, to buy.) These are substances known to disrupt the immune, endocrine and hormone systems of virtually all organisms. At the same time, the incidence of cancers among the same human population also continues to rise, along with reports of disruption to normal biological development among individuals of other species.

## Biodiversity

At the present rate of extinction, 12 per cent of bird species and 25 per cent of mammal are likely to disappear within the next thirty years.[7] As species loss continues to accelerate, it is factually uncontroversial among biologists that we are now in the midst of the sixth great extinction in the Earth's history: 1,000 to 10,000 times faster than the 'background rate' of the preceding 60 million years.[8] What is unique about this one, of course, is that it is entirely caused by a single species: us. The word 'massacre' comes to mind. It is instructive to compare the number of human beings – currently nearing 6.5 *billion*, with 250,000 more arriving every day – with the number of our fellow 'higher' mammals that still remain. Virtually all those that are large, dangerous, edible and/or profitable enough to attract our attention (or, almost as unlucky, unprofitable enough to be regarded as dispensable) now number in the tens of thousands *at very most*. There remain perhaps 414,000 great apes, all species combined, in the wild (the population of a town: Lyons, France, for example); about 8,000 tigers; guesses for African lions centre on 20,000; and in the case of most whale species, a few hundred thousand.[9] Considering a world of 11 billion people by 2150 (the 'medium-fertility' prediction), 'all of whom will continue to occupy space, drink water, burn energy, consume solid resources, produce wastes, aspire to material comfort and safety for themselves and 2.0 children, and eat', it is very hard to disagree with David Quammen: 'Call me a pessimist, but when I look into that future, I don't see any lions, tigers, or bears' (2003: 413–14). Nor, by any means, would the toll stop there.

## Habitat

The number and size of wild places – that is, those relatively unaffected by human activity – continue to decline rapidly, as development continues apace. Wild, that is, not in the unrealistically purist sense of places where there are or have been no people, but in the sense rightly suggested by David Wiggins: 'not as that which is free of all trace of our interventions . . . but as that which has not been entirely instrumentalized by human artifice, and as something to be cherished . . . in ways that outrun all considerations of profit' (2000: 10). This decline includes (but is by no means limited to) the still accelerating destruction of rainforests and coral reefs, the most biodiverse places on the planet. In fact, it is worse the biologically richer the habitat is, and thus the more species it supports. (About 50 per cent of the Earth's forests have already been cleared, and the annual net loss of forests is now 130 square miles.[10] Up to 25 per cent of coral reefs, atolls and cays have now been destroyed, and over half of the remainder are in danger of degradation beyond recovery in the next thirty years.[11])

By the 1990s, only one-third of the Earth's continental surface was left for the use of other life-forms, and by far the greater part of that in relatively impoverished or stressed ecosystems.[12] Such conversion is virtually always accompanied by gross biotic simplification towards an unsustainable monoculture. Furthermore, biologists estimate that at least 40 per cent of the Earth's ecosystems need to be protected from significant human impact in order for them to remain viable; yet only about 10 per cent are currently in a protected area (and even then, significant problems of enforcement remain).[13] It should also be noted that consumer demand for seafood has almost doubled in the last twenty years – just as wild fish stocks are crashing.[14]

These crises are, of course, all connected. So, for example, it is estimated that on average, *one-quarter* of all land animals and plants, or more than one million species, will become extinct by 2050 as a direct result of climate change.[15] The biggest danger to coral reefs is from increasing seawater acidity, also resulting from global warming; and so on. Nor does this summary exhaust the problems. For example, there is the staggering (and largely unremarked) loss of topsoil: more than 25 million acres degraded or lost annually. As Jared Diamond has said, 'There are about a dozen major environmental problems, all of them sufficiently serious that if we solved eleven of them and didn't solve the twelfth, whatever that twelfth is, any could potentially do us in.'[16]

Yet there are few signs that enough people – especially, but by no means only, among the powerful – have noticed, or care. Gregory Bateson used to point out to his students that a frog, placed in a pan of hot water, would immediately jump out; but in water that was very gradually heated, it would boil to death. He applied this story, with grim relish, to the ability of humans to notice what was happening to the environment. My only reservation is a weak

but important one: not to try to act differently, at least, is to participate in a self-fulfilling prophecy.

## Analysing Ecocrisis

As I have suggested, behind the processes driving all these human-
caused changes is not an absence of ethics but pathological ethics.
But there is also a dimension of truth or knowledge involved here.
That includes scientific knowledge, certainly, but extends well
beyond it. For the ecological crisis will not begin to change for the
better unless enough people face up to the realities I have just mentioned, both personally and collectively. There is definitely an emotional dimension to such work,[17] which is too often ignored; but
clear thinking is also required.

Before taking up ethics directly, therefore, I would like briefly to
suggest a framework for understanding the basic dynamics at
work in ecocrisis, because these make up the basic areas requiring
eco-ethical renewal. Erazim Kohak sums them up: we are too
'numerous, demanding, and powerful' (2000: 10–11). There is a
widely accepted equation for these factors: $I = P \times L \times T$.[18] That
is, our ecological I*mpact* is a function of:

> P*opulation size* (the number of humans), times
> L*ifestyle* (affluence or consumption, the per capita use of resources),
> times
> T*echnology* (the per capita effect of technologies either more or less
> energy-consuming and polluting).

(The late David Willey suggested adding another factor, namely 'O'
for the effects of the way human societies, whether micro- or
macro-, are organized, both institutionally and ideologically; hence,
PLOT.[19])

We shall look very briefly at these in turn, but first it is necessary to stress that *each* of the components is fundamental, and that
they are *interactive*. Virtually every major ecological problem is a
result of their interaction; one or another factor may predominate,

but the others can and must not be neglected, because they can wipe out any gains made by addressing solely the dominant cause. As we shall see, there are other more subtle implications, too. For example, we have (in principle) a choice between high **P** and low **L** *or* low **P** and higher **L** – at whatever level of **T** (and **O**) human wit, constrained by (among other things) the laws of physics, can achieve.

## Population

Since it is the subject of a chapter below, I won't say much about it here, except to note that global human population makes at least as significant a contribution to ecocrisis as any of the other factors. Recently the rate of *growth* has slowed, but the increase of *numbers* of new people being born has not. At a time when the Earth's ecosystemic ability to produce food and absorb wastes is already under severe strain – even for most of us, the planetary rulers – the seven billionth person is expected to arrive very shortly (2010), and a conservative estimate for 2050 is around 9 billion.[20]

## Lifestyle

Affluent overconsumption is, of course, a problem overwhelmingly present in the so-called developed world.[21] (That is not to say the developing world would necessarily behave with any more restraint given the opportunity.) It is part of the dynamic, both as result and as cause, of global corporate capitalism. Now it is not necessary to oppose capitalism as a whole – let alone markets, which are not the same thing – to realize that the extreme form that now dominates the world through its chief financial institutions (the World Trade Organization, G8, the World Bank) is having equally extreme effects: in this case, a deliberate programme to encourage consumption beyond what is desirable, let alone necessary, in human terms, or sustainable in ecological ones.

Part of this process is a cult of material consumption, now spread by the billion-dollar advertising and entertainment media industries worldwide, so that more people than ever now desire an 'American lifestyle'. The result includes some bitter ironies. It seems universally true that after a certain level of income, further increases do not lead to any more happiness. What does create discontent is the gap between the relatively poor and the rich, as perceived by the former. As a result of neo-liberal economic globalization, that is exactly what is happening: the income gap between the wealthy (who are getting richer) and the poor (who are getting poorer) is steadily increasing too. So the world is dividing into the self-indulgent wealthy, who can afford to consume irresponsibly, and do, and those who are unhappy because they would like to – and who, we are driven to hope, will not be able to.

Why 'irresponsibly'? Because those who abuse the Earth's resources by using far more than they need make up a relatively tiny minority of all people. As is well known, Americans, for example – 5 per cent of the world's people – not only emit the largest national proportion of greenhouse gases, but consume nearly 40 per cent of the Earth's natural resources (presumably excluding those several million Americans living below the poverty line.) This situation, to put it mildly, hardly seems fair. So what requires us to hope that there will be no global upgrade for everyone to the same lifestyle? Because *the Earth and its resources are finite*; so it would take at least another three planet Earths for everyone else to join the privileged few (Rees 1996: 210). This, to state the obvious, is not possible without destroying the one we actually have – not exactly an ethically defensible option.

Of course, neither is trying to keep the roughly 2 billion people now living in poverty in that condition. The only ethical option, then (to quote Arne Naess, the Deep Ecologist philosopher), is that 'We must live at a level that we seriously can wish others to attain, not at a level that requires the bulk of humanity NOT to reach' (quoted in Witoszek and Brennan 1999: 224). There would be no need to choose between social injustice and ecological suicide if the wealthy minority were to reduce their consumption – and only to a level which would still enable a reasonably comfortable 'European' lifestyle (at the modest end of the spectrum) – while the majority increase theirs enough to permit the same. (Nor would it be necessary for the majority to live at low consumption levels if the total number of people was smaller, however.)

These eventualities are surely at least *possible*. So, however madly optimistic it may sound at the moment, let us assume that sufficient integrity, will and intelligence, on the part of both political and other leaders and the public, can still be found to institute a programme of reduced consumption in time for it to matter. That is an enormous challenge, some aspects of which will be discussed below.

All this said, there is a tendency for environmentalists on the left to grant transnational companies even more power than they actually have (and thereby neglect other aspects of the $I = PLOT$ equation). They are a huge part, but ultimately only part, of the problem, and therefore only part of the challenge. Companies are driven by, as well as drive, many aspects of the economic and social environment in which they work. They are a symptom of the problem as well as a cause, being importantly products of, for example, the economic environment, government fiscal policy, trade regulation or lack thereof and (not least) both the greed and the ignorance of many of their customers as well as of their directors and shareholders. Since we are not going to get very far unless we tackle the causes as well as the symptoms of ecocrisis, these too are things which must be faced up to. For example, just appealing to the ecological conscience of corporate producers and consumers and instituting purely voluntary controls will certainly fail; but for tougher measures to succeed, there has to be at least some degree of general cultural understanding and support for them.


Technology


Let me remind you of the interactivity of these factors. So, for example, even in the decidedly optimistic scenario just described, unless overall consumption declines markedly (and stays that way), the issues of technology and population cannot simply be ignored. And it bears repeating that if the number of people on the planet increases sufficiently, then no amount of progress in reducing consumption *or* instituting green technology will suffice.

Many people, including those in most governments, place their faith in new technologies as the solution to every present and indeed future ecological problem. And it is true that appropriate, clean and affordable technology has an important role to play in resolving the ecocrisis; but it cannot bear the weight of cornucopian dreams. Technology is vanishingly unlikely to be able to compensate for uncontrolled expansion of either population or consumption. For example, it tends to become increasingly expensive and/or specialized, and technological 'solutions' notoriously tend to create new problems, which then seem to require more technological intervention – and so on. Still more fundamentally, such 'solutions' to ecological problems lock us into a collective mindset – run by techno-science, financed by capital and protected by state power – which is a principal cause of those problems. Then that cause can only be perceived, with increasingly desperate denial, as the only solution.

Let us assume that cheap and efficient non-polluting technologies were in fact developed and made widely available. If they were simply used to license massive increases in consumption – i.e., if they were not accompanied by a (successful) attempt to control and reduce *demand*, and thus consumption – then the end result would just be the same. Indeed, abundant cheap energy could well be an absolute disaster from an ecocentric point of view, if it were used to advance even further human domination and exploitation of the planet – even if the profits were fairly divided up among the conquerors. (Which seems more unlikely? That they *would* be so divided, or that such a discovery *wouldn't* be used for that end? Hard to say!)

It is also worth pointing out, against the more optimistic exponents of future techno-fixes, that while technology develops with certain advances in scientific knowledge, it is presumably still constrained by the laws of physics. Doubtless, our understanding of physics will continue to grow, but it seems unreasonable to rely on developing technology which requires what we know of the underlying behaviour of the universe to change also.

In short, as Kohak writes, 'the Earth cannot be saved by even the most perfect technocratic scheme if ordinary citizens do not themselves realize the need for a basic change in the way we dwell upon this Earth, confront the apostle of consumption and find the will to live in sustainable ways' (2000: xxvi).


## Science and Technology


Belief in technological fixes is symptomatic of a wider faith in modern techno-science. (The term is justified: it is becoming ever-increasingly difficult to distinguish between science and technology.[22]) Actually, that faith has recently been shaken by nuclear accidents and BSE ('mad cow disease')/vCJD (its human version), as the cool public response to GM foods, in Europe at least, seems to show. Even so, techno-science is now integral to both industry and government (with those two also becoming ever closer).[23] In the 'West', at least, it has now become so powerful and dogmatic as to constitute, in effect, a secular religion with its own powerful and democratically unaccountable elite.[24] And as with other major institutionalized religions, this social, political and economic power involves a self-justifying ideology that can and must be questioned.

For example, the belief that science arrives at the final or complete truth of anything – including such refinements as 'eventually', or 'as close to it as we can ever get' – is ultimately nothing more or less than an article of faith, requiring sweeping prior assumptions that cannot themselves be scientifically tested. (Not, that is, without already assuming the truth of science.)[25] More specific tenets of the scientific faith can also be questioned: that there is such a thing as *the* scientific method, for example;[26] or that replication – repeating experiments – guarantees the truth of their outcome.

Nonetheless, the idea that science offers unique access to 'the truth' has widespread rhetorical plausibility, even among those whose interests are damaged by its exercise. (The word for such a phenomenon is **hegemony**.) Even when there is no *scientific* support for it,[27] when this plausibility is embodied in official institutions and the general culture it lends techno-science great political, social and cultural power. And to these points can be added the corruption of science by the politics and especially money with which it is now so entangled.[28]

Yet absolutely none of this is to deny that science can supply us with very important *truths* (lower-case 't', and plural), nor that it has a rightful place in our ongoing cultural conversation. These criticisms are not 'anti-science', they are anti-*scientism*: the modern cult of science, according to which science is not one way of being among many but the *only* valid or true one.[29] As Paul Feyerabend remarked, 'The objection that [a] scenario is "real," and that we must adapt to it no matter what, has no weight: there are many ways of thinking and living' (1995: 164). (This point has important implications for any project to bring about a more ecological society, which we shall explore later.)

For several reasons, this situation presents a particular problem for ecological ethics. One is that the science of ecology was, of course, a major inspiration for metaphysical and political ecology. Another is that science plays a massive part in our awareness of the fact of ecocrisis; it supplies many of the indicators outside of our personal experience, and virtually all of the quantifiable and statistical ones. Furthermore, it is needed to underpin the limited but important role of green technology in alleviating that crisis. So its importance is clear.

Yet there are also cogent reasons why techno-science does not itself offer a solution to the ecocrisis. Indeed, paradoxically, the value that proponents of science place on 'objectivity' can contribute to the ecocrisis as much as, in another way, it can help by gathering, analysing and presenting evidence. Why? One reason is the extent to which an overemphasis in this respect, and a corresponding devaluation of the value of the Earth in its sensuous particulars and emotional meanings – 'things' that do not survive being quantified or, significantly, commodified – is itself implicated in that crisis. Relatedly, it is highly doubtful that reason *alone*, scientific or otherwise, will suffice to save the Earth; that will take emotion as well as intellect – and probably, as we shall see, spirituality (of a particular kind).

Another reason is that in a society dominated by financial, commercial and fiscal imperatives, science is no more immune than any other human enterprise to the corruption entailed by selling your services to the highest bidder. Not only are the subjects of research largely dictated by their potential profits, but experimental results are themselves increasingly influenced by the interests of corporate funding.[30]

More subtly, an apparently purely scientific approach lends itself too readily to a 'sensible consensus' in which those interests are concealed and made difficult to question because such questions are deemed to be unscientific and therefore, conveniently, illegitimate. But this is precisely the most serious problem with techno-science. It cannot supply answers to the kinds of question that most urgently need asking: questions of meaning, value and justice. Its strength is also necessarily its weakness, because in order to be 'objective' science must set aside as 'subjective' precisely such questions. Science might be able to tell us (subject to the appropriate qualifications) what is currently considered 'true', but it cannot tell us what is *good, or right, or fair*. These are not, and cannot be, scientific questions; nor are they questions that should be left to scientists or other 'experts' to decide; they are existential decisions we must make for ourselves.[31]

This conclusion does not entail abandoning science but qualifying and recontextualizing it. I believe, with Bruno Latour, that 'The critical mind, if it is to be relevant again, must devote itself to the cultivation of a stubborn realism, but a realism dealing with what I will call matters of concern, not matters of fact.'[32] And what more deserving matter of concern is there, calling for just such a stubborn realism, than the fate of the Earth?

# 3

## *Ethics*

## What is Ethics?

'Ethics' comes from the Greek word *ethos*, meaning custom, but in its proper philosophical usage it now refers not to how people actually *do* behave in their dealings with each other, but to how they *ought* to behave.[1] It is a complex and controversial subject, both as a branch of philosophy and in its various 'applications' (such as in medicine, law and now 'the environment'). The fundamental ethical question, which I have already mentioned Socrates as posing, is how should one best live, or what should one best do? At least three points follow.

1 Questions of value – whose study is called ***axiology*** – are unavoidable. Ethics concerns the realization of values (both in the sense of 'realizing what they are' and of 'making them real'). For example, philosophers argue about what sort of entities qualify as ***morally considerable*** – that is, have moral standing. Some characteristic (or set of characteristics) is required to confer this status. It is usually one they agree is possessed by humans, such as sentience or self-consciousness; its bearers are thus

granted membership as honorary humans. But the qualifying
characteristic is only relevant because it is deemed to have value.

2   Particular instances of individual right and wrong behaviour –
    which are often described as instances of **morality** – are import-
    ant, but they are only a subset of ethics as a whole.

3   Ultimately, private ethics is secondary to public, for three
    reasons. First, what finally matters, insofar as it has direct effects
    upon the world (including other beings), is not private states of
    being but public behaviour. Second, human beings are highly,
    perhaps even necessarily, social animals; so private ethics is cru-
    cially affected by public. And third, much of ethics necessarily
    concerns constraints on the activities of individuals for the
    common good of the communities of which they are a part, and
    upon which they depend. (But, to anticipate a point made
    below, those communities should no longer be restricted to
    purely human ones.[2])

Finally, ethics also overlaps with questions of knowledge, such as
how we actually know – or at least, decide – what has value and
what is good behaviour, the study of which is called **epistemology**.
So we now turn to an overview of epistemological issues that
impact upon ethics.[3]

## Ethical Realism vs. Relativism

**Realism** is basically the view that there are things, values or ways of
behaving that exist independently of whether anyone knows them
(in any way) – often put as being 'really there', or 'out there' –
which are therefore real; the accuracy of our knowledge of them,
as representations of realities, can therefore be judged – at least in
principle – the way one would compare copies with an original.
Therefore, a representation which matches its original reality in
every relevant respect is the truth. Science is usually held to be the
best exemplar of this process, which is also therefore described as
'objective'. Realists are therefore almost always also **objectivists** (and
are happy to call themselves such).

***Relativism*** is basically the counter-view that: whether or not there are 'things in themselves', some things (and arguably all things) can never actually be known in themselves, because they can never be separated from our knowledge of them (perception, conception, etc.); therefore, 'representations' can only ever be compared with other 'representations', never with an unrepresented reality; there are, therefore, and can be, only truths which are relative in the sense that they are not final, complete or absolute. This view, sometimes described as 'subjective', has a strong affinity with the humanities and arts. Relativists are therefore often called ***subjectivists***. (However, since this tends to be used as a term of abuse in a society which places great value on 'objectivity', it is a label many relativists resist.)

It is important to understand that both positions are open to abuse; indeed, both are widely misunderstood, sometimes even by those who seem to advocate them.

Realism – the *effort* to be objective – certainly has its place as a valid and valuable *ideal*, and the experience of closing in on the truth, so to speak, is an integral part of it. But the relativists have a valid point, at least respecting loose talk about objective truth and/or reality. As one of them puts it, 'the "truth", factual or otherwise, about the being of objects is constituted within a theoretical and discursive context, and the idea of a truth outside all context is simply nonsensical' (Laclau 1991: 105). This is because neither objects nor facts – let alone concepts or values – exist *for* us except insofar as they are apprehended *by* us, and that apprehension is necessarily inseparable from the processes of learning (such as what qualifies as a thing or a fact, and all further gradations) that have made it possible. Furthermore, no one has a 'view from nowhere' (Nagel 1986); everyone's apprehension is necessarily from a particular biologically embodied and socially embedded perspective.

On the other hand, relativism is commonly portrayed (by realists) as suggesting that since (a) absolute truth is impossible, (b) there is no such thing as truth *at all*, and that any representation or statement therefore has as much or little truth as any other. This is indeed absurd, but it is hard to find anyone who actually holds such a view. In any case, (b) does not follow from (a) unless one *assumes* an absolutist definition of truth.[4] More broadly, truth results from

ongoing processes of perceiving and conceiving animals in continuous interaction with the world. Even in its most stable forms truth
therefore cannot be taken to be complete or final; but that certainly
does not mean there is no such thing at all. Indeed, we cannot live
our daily lives without some notion of what is true and what isn't,
let alone practise a higher cultural form such as science (or, for that
matter, art).

In short, everything we can know, think about, or discuss –
including ethics – is a function *both* of the 'objective' world *and* of
our 'subjective' apprehension of it. And the resulting knowledge
is converted, through the same processes of awareness, reflection
and interaction, into decisions (both individual and collective) for
action.

We may therefore legitimately speak of facts, understood as
truths at the present time and in relation to particular, not universal, circumstances; but claims by scientific spokespersons of objectivity (held to be superior to subjectivity) and realism (as superior to
relativism) should be rejected, and viewed as essentially rhetorical
and political interventions. Equally unacceptable, however, are the
interventions of vulgar relativists along the lines of, 'Well that's just
your opinion. Mine is different and that's all there is to it.' Such a
move kills off debate (reasons, arguments, etc.) just at the point
when it is most needed. It is, of course, an argument itself, and a
bad one.[5]

## The Naturalistic Fallacy

This term refers to the important point that no single ethical position (i.e., prescription: what should be) logically follows from any
set of facts (i.e., description: what is). Or, as philosophers tend to
put it, you cannot legitimately derive an 'ought' from an 'is'.[6]
Indeed, it is hard enough to derive an 'is' (general conclusion) from
an 'is' (as a set of empirical data). Not only is it impossible to collect
data without criteria that embody assumptions that are not themselves subject to 'testing', but it is always possible to interpret the
same set of facts in more than one way, and thereby arrive at very

different conclusions.[7] Furthermore, in daily practice there is no clear-cut distinction between what we consider a fact and what we value; the two constantly interact in both directions.[8]

In relation to the naturalistic fallacy, however, the fundamental point is that ethics and facts are two different orders of discourse. There is no (good) reason to think that just because a behaviour is 'natural' – say, the persecution of an outsider by a group – it is therefore ethically correct. The latter is a different and, for ethics, more important question, and it should be decided on other grounds.

True, it is valuable to have an idea of our so-called natures: how we tend to respond to certain situations, what we tend to value, and so on. This sort of attention to our biological 'hard-wiring' is especially the province of sociobiology and evolutionary psychology. But (as I suggested earlier) such knowledge cannot answer the hard ethical questions we face, and thereby replace ethics. Even if subordinating everything to professional status, or producing ten children, or eating a high-meat diet are indeed 'natural' behaviours, are they good or right?[9] That, once again, is a very different question.

This is not to say (as a dogmatic realist might) that no sound ethical conclusions at all are possible, or (as a dogmatic relativist might) that any ethical position has as much or little validity as any other. The fallacy is the attempt to use facts about what is 'natural' to justify a *particular* ethic as 'good'. But it does not invalidate *all* attempts to arrive at a defensible ethic; it just means that the attempt must proceed on different grounds, such as arguments as to what is needed, desirable, and so on.

Ethics actually exists in that uncomfortable place between what is and what ought to be. It cannot be solely concerned with 'what ought to be' in any sense that excludes 'what is', because the former is a kind of imaginal[10] 'what is', and nonetheless important or even real on that account. Furthermore, if 'what is' (presently) is ignored, then the prospects of realizing 'what ought to be' are even more hopeless than usual. But equally, ethics cannot be limited to 'what is'. Evolutionary psychology, at least in its populist form, increasingly lays claim to 'what is', and then attempts to derive an ethics that conforms to its view. The result, deprived of philosophical substance and shackled to a passing intellectual and ideological fashion, is a poor substitute for the real thing.

# Religious Ethics

Virtually all ethics began, and for most of human history has persisted, as *religious* codes of behaviour. There is wide variation, of course, but such codes are derived from interacting with either local spirits (animism), various deities (polytheism), the nature of sacred reality itself (Buddhist nontheism) or, most influentially, God Himself through the words of His prophets and/or incarnations (Judaic, Christian and Islamic theism).

It is worth noting that, philosophically speaking, ethics itself cannot be derived directly from a deity, no matter how apparently authoritative or comprehensive. The reason is that 'Should I obey the commands of this deity?' is a valid ethical question, and arguably an unavoidable one.[11] However, perhaps not surprisingly, this point has not received much encouragement among religious adherents.

In the 'West' – and much of the rest of the globe, as a result of colonialism, including globalization, during the last 300 years – the most influential kind of religious ethics has been Christianity. Ecologically speaking, it is a mixed legacy at best. According to the New Testament, Jesus praised the lilies of the field (Matthew 7: 28–9); but he also blasted a fig tree for failing to feed him (Mark 11: 12–14, 20–1), and his use of a herd of pigs to dispose of two demons (Matthew 8: 28–32) was disturbingly casual at best.

In any case, the foundational text in this context has always been Genesis 1: 26, 28, which states what has come to be known as the *dominion thesis*:

> And God said unto them, Let us make man in our image, after our likeness, and let them have dominion over the fish of the sea, and over the fowl of the air, and over the cattle, and over all the earth, and over every creeping thing that creepeth upon the earth. . . . And God said unto them, Be fruitful, and multiply, and replenish the earth, and subdue it: and have dominion over the fish of the sea, and over the fowl of the air, and over every living thing that moveth upon the earth.

In 1967, Lynn White Jr. wrote a short article pointing out that this passage had been overwhelmingly, and understandably, interpreted as giving humans the right to do whatever they want to the Earth and all its non-human inhabitants, subject only to God's approval – in practice, rarely, it seems, a stringent test. He also pointed out – again, correctly – that with the insistence on a single, transcendent and universal God, Christianity (and, by implication, Islam) had removed the sacred focus from the Earth and its creatures. For pagan animists, nature itself had been sacred; an essentially off-planet deity, in contrast, amounted to a potential licence to plunder. White went on to suggest that Christianity is therefore the primary historical cause of ecological crisis.

However plausible, this suggestion was exposed to criticism on the good grounds that (1) quite other interpretations of the Bible are possible; (2) pre-Christian humanity also engaged in many bouts of ecological destructiveness (mass felling of forests, the hunting of some megafauna to extinction, etc.); (3) non-Christian people have done the same; and (4) the ecocrisis didn't really gather pace until the Industrial Revolution in the nineteenth century. However, such points, while true, have tended to obscure another one: that whether or not the 'real' message of Christianity is ecologically despotic or not (something that could be debated indefinitely), that is in fact *how it has commonly and influentially been understood*.[12]

There is an alternative interpretation of the Bible known as the **stewardship thesis**, based on Genesis 1: 24 and 2: 15:[13]

> And God made the beast of the earth after his kind, and the cattle after their kind, and every thing that creepeth upon the earth after their kind: and God saw that it was good. . . . And the Lord took the man [i.e., Adam], and put him into the garden of Eden to dress it and to keep it.

According to this benevolent reading, humanity can use the natural world but only with due regard for the fact that God created it and gave us responsibility for its well-being. This provides an opportunity for Christian environmentalists to try to put ecology onto the churches' agenda. And that is indeed a good thing, which should be wished every success. Practically, however, it would be unwise to weigh it down with too heavy a freight of hope. Compared to the great bulk of that agenda, which remains strongly anthropocentric, green stewardship remains a distinctly minority concern, and still has a long way to go – although that is not a good reason not to try to develop it, of course.

Stewardship also has a problem of substance: it is distinctly paternalistic. Does nature actually need us to guide or manage it? Surely we need the Earth much more than it needs us. And that weakness makes it a close cousin (perhaps ancestor?) to one of the curses of our time: *managerialism*, or the belief that human beings have not only the 'right' but the ability, even if only potentially, to successfully manage the natural world. Given our overall historical record for successfully managing even ourselves, plus our all-too-human susceptibility to narrow and short-term self-interest, this prospect is open to serious doubt. It might just be possible – but only if the managers accept that no amount of knowledge will ever suffice without the wisdom to recognize its limits, and ours.[14] (This is a point, by the way, with which most ecotheologians would agree.)

## Secular Ethics

With the modern world – beginning, for most intents and purposes, in the mid-seventeenth century – *secular* ethics became increasingly important. (There were earlier precedents; the French writer Michel de Montaigne suggested in the late sixteenth century that while the most serious Christian sins were offences against God, our worst crimes were actually against each other – and animals.[15])

The process of secularization has been slow, uneven and notably incomplete, even in the 'West', but broadly speaking it took place like this. With the rise of the philosophy known as *humanism* in and soon after the Renaissance in the sixteenth century, man (although not, until much later, woman) increasingly began to replace divinity as the central focus of life. At the same time, secular natural truth took the place of God as the ultimate goal, and human reason played the part once given to divine revelation as the means to attain it. Originally itself religious, in the eighteenth-century

Enlightenment, humanism became increasingly, and more openly, secular, and God an increasingly hands-off figure who no longer interfered in the universe He had set, like a clock, to working. Public atheism finally became possible in the nineteenth century.

Note, however, the profound continuities with monotheism, namely the monist logic: there is still only one legitimate source of meaning ('truth'), with only one legitimate caste of interpreters. As reason itself became steadily replaced by scientific and technical reason, in the course of the Scientific Revolution (which really was revolutionary),[16] that caste eventually became the authorities in white coats we still, however uneasily, recognize today. Here a distinction must be made between genuine science itself and, as already mentioned, scientism – science as a faith in, or even cult of, reason.[17] The latter is yet another example of how much secular-ism still functions as a crypto-religion; true scepticism is also self-critical.[18]

The original Renaissance philosophy about the importance of human initiative within divine and natural limits thus mutated into an arrogant techno-humanism which now recognizes none.[19] Its followers, sometimes called **cornucopians**, believe that there is no serious problem which does not have a scientific/technological solution, and no end to human progress and growth. The latter tends, it seems, to merge with economics and so-called economic reason (hence, **economism**). According to this faith, what matters most is literally business as usual, only ever more so, according to the logic of the cancer cell: endless growth.

It may be argued that philosophers such as Descartes, Newton and Kant, who helped create the modern world and were in turn created by it, had no such intention. Perhaps so, but as with the Bible, what has mattered more is the dominant (mis)understanding and (ab)use of their ideas. The result of that has been to contribute to a powerfully held view of the non-human natural world as a set of inert raw resources to be mastered and exploited by human reason. In relation to much the greater part of humanity's existence, for which nature was also subject and agent, this is a very recent and drastic change.

In the course of this process, ethics as a subject was transformed from a branch of theology into a secular philosophical discourse, with the focus not on divinity but on human relations. The price, however, was that ethics itself became increasingly a matter of mere technical intellectual expertise, confined to university departments: one speciality among many.

If ethics was no longer predominantly religious, how did it connect with the so-called real world? Or, to put it another way, what world(s) did it now take in? Modern secular ethics divides largely into two concerns, which we shall examine more closely next: the individual rights of liberal democracy, and the collective rights of social/socialist democracy. But in both cases, the guarantor of rights is the state, with which individuals and/or groups supposedly have a contract: they cede the state its power in return for its protection of them and their rights. (The dominant philosopher of this *statism* was Thomas Hobbes.)[20]

Despite the control over it that democracy is supposed to exert, however, the state itself is increasingly run – and its ethics determined – by the power of capital and its principal representatives, transnational companies, together with the science and technology from which both states and capital are increasingly inseparable. The best name for this entire process is *modernism*. The term does not refer here to a school of artistic, architectural or other such thought, but to the nexus of ideas and values – centred on the interlocking institutions of capital, techno-science and the nation-state – that drive the project of modernity.[21] Socially and historically speaking, then, this is the 'environment' which gave birth to modern ethics. To question the latter, as increasing numbers of people are now doing, and as we are doing here, is therefore also to question that project. In that sense, at least, it is postmodern.

# 4

## Three Schools of Ethics

Broadly speaking, there are three schools of ethics in philosophy. (One could also call them 'traditions', except that two are modern.) It is important for our purposes to know something of them, since they provide much of the intellectual part of any contemporary context for discussing ethics. It is equally important, however, to realize their limitations, particularly ecological. The following discussion is therefore framed by ecological ethics; it is not meant to be an exhaustive treatment of each school in itself.

## Virtue Ethics

Virtue ethics is by far the oldest of the three, stemming largely from the philosophy of Plato, especially as developed by Aristotle (384–322 BCE). Its central focus is on *developing a virtuous character*, such that good or right actions result naturally from its dispositions. Conversely, the exercise of virtue is what produces a good person. Such a character is marked by its possession of the four classical virtues: temperance, justice, courage and (practical) wisdom. (Contrast these with the later and very different Christian virtues of faith, hope and charity.) These attributes constitute what Aristotle called *eudaimonia*, which is often translated as 'happiness'. A better rendition, however, would be 'well-being', including not only living well but doing well.

The emphasis on character is not as individualistic as it sounds to us, for a number of reasons. In this tradition, humans are seen as integrally social and political animals; thus, *eudaimonia* cannot be developed in isolation. Furthermore, by the same token, a person who embodies it will also promote it among others. Also (and this is a point of potential ecological importance), although Aristotle and his successors clearly had other human beings in mind, there is nothing in the theory itself limiting who or what can be the object of virtuous behaviour.

Virtue ethics has been criticized as potentially circular – a character is defined in terms of the virtues, which are defined by that character – and **teleological**. That means having and/or being defined by a predetermined goal (*telos* in Greek), which Aristotle called a *final cause*. The two aspects are related: behaviour is taken as determined by goals, which are inferred from behaviours. Teleology has been distinctly out of philosophical favour for the last 350 years; much of the knowledge resulting from modern science (especially biology) was, in part, the result of abandoning whatever had already been decided was the purpose of, say, an organism, in favour of examining what Aristotle would have called its *efficient cause*(s): what is 'driving' or 'pushing' rather than 'pulling' it into its particular existence. Typically, however, this movement went too far and tried to banish consideration of purpose altogether. True, it is difficult (some philosophers think impossible) to give a causal account of how 'subjective' purposes result in 'objective' behaviour; but that does not mean organisms do not have goals, or that they do not matter. In short, this criticism of virtue ethics is not impossible to overcome with a less ambitious and more limited – but still real – version of purpose.

The attack on virtue ethics just mentioned was part of the reason for its almost wholesale eclipse in modern philosophy, until fairly recently, when it has been developed in ways that do not depend on Aristotle's teleology. Its promise has now even been noted specifically in connection with ecology.[1] But before we come to that, the two schools which overtook it, both with their origins in the late eighteenth century, are as follows.

## Deontology ('Rights')

Deontological ethics takes its name from the Greek *to deon*, meaning duty, or 'that which must be done' (rather than 'is simply an option'). To put it another way, actions fulfilling duty are morally right regardless of their consequences. Its modern founder was Immanuel Kant (1724–1804), a complex and difficult philosopher whose work does not lend itself to ready summary.[2]

Where Aristotle had found the goal of ethics to be 'happiness', Kant concluded it was duty. But more immediately, he was reacting against the earlier assertion by David Hume that ethical behaviour is, in the end, not a matter of reasons, or even reason as such, but of people's sympathy and emotion, or what he called 'passions', respecting the individual cases which they encounter. (Hume reserved reason for logic and mathematics.) Kant was determined to come up with a rational definition of ethics, whose principles would be *categorical* (unconditional and, as such, binding for any rational being) and *universal* (apply without any exceptions). Such principles would therefore compel the agreement of every rational being.

Kant's solution to this challenge was to propose a 'categorical imperative', the two principal aspects or formulations of which are as follows: (1) act only on a maxim that you can will at the same time to be or become a universal law; and since such maxims can only (he thought) be discovered by autonomous agents who are both the agents and source of value; (2) treat all people as ends or subjects in their own right and never merely as means or objects only.[3] These injunctions were meant to be followed regardless of the specific consequences (for oneself or others).

One implication is that good *intentions* are all-important. Another is that so too is *duty*, including specific duties, as (in principle) infallible guides to how to behave and what to do. And from both principles together follows the idea of universal *individual human rights*. Duties and rights are ultimately inseparable, because your duty to treat the other person as you would wish to be treated is his or her right to be treated thus, and vice versa. The name **contractarianism** comes from the idea that the only role of the state, as a limited if legitimate collectivity, is to guarantee and enforce people's rights. But note that both rights and duties are, at least in Kant's intention, limited to human beings as supposedly the only rational animals, and are purely individual.

Not surprisingly, given its rationalism, deontological ethics has come to dominate academic philosophy, especially as developed by the work of the late John Rawls, and legal philosophy. More broadly, its focus on duties, in a culture increasingly dominated by rights alone, is welcome, and it embodies some important truths with an intellectually satisfying elegance. But its weaknesses result from the same emphases, and are at least equally serious in an ecological context.

To begin with, it is questionable to what extent Kant's answer to Hume's challenge was successful. The 'passions' play as large a role in our lives as ever, and reason is by no means necessarily the most important or even distinctive human attribute; it is certainly not an absolute attribute. (Reasoning is, finally, increasingly admitted to be present in other species as well.) Similarly, people have many other values and reference points than reason, or rights. Again, in practice – notwithstanding 'universal reason' – both rights and rules can and do conflict, and it is merely an assertion of faith that there is always a higher principle to appeal to which will resolve the conflict. We might also remark that neither reason nor duty is proof against the fact that 'people's consciences can be as perverted as anything else' (Blackburn 2001: 19). In fact, as Schopenhauer observed, not only can 'reasonable' and 'vicious' be mutually consistent but 'only through their union are great and far-reaching crimes possible'.[4]

Much of the substance of these problems stems from the underlying fact that rationality, in this theory, is extraordinarily abstract. Even the beings concerned are abstract ones, insofar as deontological ethics is entirely anti-empirical and supposedly rests on a priori principles, i.e., ones not derived from personal experience. Radically isolated from the embodied and substantive ways actual persons live and experience their lives, 'rational' easily becomes circular: those who agree to these rational principles are therefore rational people, and the principles are considered to be rational because those people agree that they are. Meanwhile, in practice, it ends up referring to an elite restricted not only to humans but also mainly males, mainly whites, mainly members of the professional middle class, and mainly 'Western'.

It is true that one's categorical duty might well be to protect nature, for example. But nature here is understood as a passive and inferior recipient of any such protection; it is not an agent and thus an equal, because it is not 'rational'. As a believer in rationalism, Kant was unable to supply any substantive reason as to why, as supposedly non-rational beings, even animals, let alone the rest of nature, should be treated well – except as practice for treating humans well! (Schopenhauer was scathing on this point.[5]) In this important sense, deontology is decidedly anthropocentric. Rawls confirms this: the 'status of the natural world and our proper relation to it is not a constitutional essential or a basic question of justice', and any beliefs pertaining to the non-human world, no matter how 'considered', are 'outside the scope of the theory of justice' (Rawls 1993: 246, 448). The just community, it seems, is reserved for humanity alone.

Rationalist deontology, as developed by Rawls and his peers, has also become academic in the unflattering sense. However influential within the academy, from a more broadly and deeply engaged perspective it appears largely divorced from life in practice: scholastic, hyper-abstract, and with correspondingly little to show in positive political influence.[6]

Deontology *has* achieved considerable social and political influence with the idea of rights or, at least, the common understanding thereof. (Hitherto, at least, these have been very largely human rights). It is possible to value such rights while also being aware of the limitations. In relation to ecological ethics, there are at least two. One, ironically, is the tendency to disassociate rights from corresponding duties. (This is a result of the triumph of the modern liberal version of rights over the older republican version; the latter, significantly, is closely related to Aristotelian virtue ethics.[7]) The second flaw is individualism, which leaves questions of the common good – not exactly unimportant – dangerously unattended.

Some philosophers, notably Tom Regan, have extended deontology to animals, arguing that as beings with interests they too
qualify for treatment as ends in themselves, not just as means to
human ends. This has resulted in the influential *animals rights move-*
*ment*. As we shall see later, others, such as Paul Taylor, have tried to
extend the same theory even to (individual) plants. But this attempt
suffers from many of the same defects just noted. In any case, for
the reasons just listed, it is difficult to see how a fully ecological
ethics could be developed while still remaining within the deontological fold.

## Utilitarianism ('Consequences')

The chief modern competing school of ethics is that of **consequen-**
**tialism**, according to which 'the value of an action' – and thence its
ethical character – 'derives entirely from the value of its consequences' (Blackburn 1994: 77). This view is the opposite of what
deontologists assert. Its dominant form, founded by Jeremy Bentham
(1748–1832) and further developed by John Stuart Mill (1806–73),
holds that the highest good, and therefore the ultimate ethical
criterion, is the greatest happiness – itself defined as pleasure – of the
greatest number of people. In other words, the decisive ethical
question about an action is whether or not it is useful in relation to
the general happiness of humanity. For that reason, this school is also
known as **utilitarianism**. (Confusingly, it is also often described as
teleological, because actions are judged in relation to the preset goal
of happiness.)

There are two kinds of utilitarian ethics: *hedonistic*, in which a
general definition of happiness (decided, in practice, by the relevant
'experts') is applied; and *preference*, in which the goal is to maximize
not pleasure but the satisfaction of preferences which people are
permitted to define for themselves. The last kind is certainly more
democratic; however, it should also be noted that such utilitarians
make it difficult to criticize what those preferences actually are.[8] No
matter how heinous what makes someone happy may be, this
school, as such, has little to say about it. Note too that preferences

often conflict, and are therefore not susceptible to a final ordering without one particular kind being imposed (ultimately, arbitrarily) as the highest or best kind.

Some important general points follow. One is that for conse-quentialists/utilitarians – and this sharply marks them out from the preceding school – the subjective motivations of objective actions are irrelevant; it doesn't matter if the right thing is done for the 'wrong' reason, or vice versa. This results in a tendency to dismiss motivation as irrelevant – something that does not follow from the plausible belief that results are ultimately more important. And that position is attractive. If taken to be in any way absolute, however, it is vulnerable to the reply the late twentieth-century Chinese politician Chou En-lai gave when asked what he thought were the consequences of the French Revolution: 'It's too soon to tell.' There is a serious point behind the quip: since utilitarianism can only judge the correctness of actions after the fact, in order for it to help make decisions an assumption is necessary along the lines of 'based on predicted outcomes' or 'given past occurrences it is probable that . . .'[9]

Also in contrast to the deontologists, consequentialism is ulti-mately collective. True, individual experiences matter – but only, in the end, to enable totting up a final tally of general happiness; if the latter clearly outweighs a few of the former, it is too bad for them. Social well-being trumps individual rights. Consequentialism thus has a potential political affinity with collectivist politics, whether of the 'right' (authoritarian/fascist) or 'left' (collectivist-socialist).

Notice too that happiness has to be susceptible to being 'objec-tively' measured; otherwise, it cannot be calculated, or outcomes compared. For the same reason, it must be 'universal'; if there are substantively different happinesses, they may be *incommensurable* (i.e., incapable of being compared), and then the system would break down. As a result, utilitarians tend to measure that which can be measured and ignore that which cannot; or, relatedly, they redefine something that cannot be measured as something that can, and then use that (without changing its name) to replace the awkward original. This problem is further compounded by its vulnerability to a few powerful people deciding what 'general happiness' consists of, and giving the result a spurious air of objective and universal truth. (Indeed, happiness is not even necessarily every-one's overriding goal.)

Putting these points together, it is hardly surprising that utilitar-ianism is the most powerful single philosophy in social and eco-nomic policy in the modern 'Western' world. That is, utilitarianism's emphasis on objectivity, on collectivity and on measurement is a fundamental part of the modern project; but so too, sadly and often even tragically, are its flaws.[10]

As we shall see, utilitarianism has been influentially extended to animals by Peter Singer, following on from Bentham's famous asser-tion that 'The question is not, can they *reason*? Nor, can they *talk*? But can they *suffer*?' (1907: ch. 17, sec. 1, fn. to para 4). This point is very well taken, but Singer's programme does not entirely escape the problems just mentioned. Together with the animal rights school, the resulting *animal liberation movement* (largely inspired by Singer) is achieving admirably practical results in improving animal welfare; and it has helped that he has largely dropped the illusion that what matters most can be measured. But it remains vulnerable to anyone claiming that the collective human happiness resulting from, say, factory farming, outweighs the suffering of the animals themselves.

Its greatest ecological weakness, however, results from the unavoidable utilitarian position that 'actions are right or wrong, good or bad, according to how they affect the experiences of beings capable of experience' (Wenz 2001: 85). In other words, utilitar-ianism requires – and is limited to – *sentience*, or rather, *sentient beings*. (This doesn't contradict the collectivist emphasis just noted; sentience is a prerequisite for it.) A being without sentience cannot (apparently) suffer, or experience pleasure, or have preferences; so about a non-sentient being – a species, for example, or an ecosys-tem, or a place – utilitarians have, again, little to say.

These three ethical philosophies overlap. Indeed, in practice they cannot ultimately be separated. For example, it is plausible to see 'maximizing the good of the greatest number' as a universal rule and duty; motives for actions (especially insofar as they influence the choice of means) usually have a significant effect on their outcomes; and the successful realization of rules for realizing the good requires, and results in, a kind of virtue, and the accumulation of virtues (or vices) results in a kind of character.

In fact, *all* the considerations characteristically emphasized by each school – motivations for actions as well as their effects, rules for behaviour but also their inculcation as virtue – are important. The fine distinctions academics often draw between them are therefore ultimately of questionable value. But note something else, too, that they share: all three are concerned overwhelmingly with human beings and their interrelationships. As Sylvan and Bennett note, 'environmentally at least, all established ethics are inadequate' (1994: 26). Of course there have been attempts to move established ethics in an ecological direction: how successfully, we shall see.

# 5

## *Value*

## Some Issues

I have already said that there can be no ethics without value, the study of which is called 'axiology'. In this section, therefore, we are going to look more closely at the nature of value, especially as it concerns the natural world.

Value can be held to inhere in either single, discrete items, in which case it is *individualist*, or in sets of such items, in which case it is *holist*. The usual example of the former is an individual person, animal or living being; the latter may include species or biotic places, comprising (at a minimum) two or more individuals who are connected in some non-random or arbitrary way – with species, genetically, or with places, ecosystemically.

A still more important distinction is between *instrumental value* and *intrinsic value*. The first kind is the value someone or something has as a *means* to something else, where that something else constitutes, in effect, a good in itself (or, at least, is more valued than the means). In contrast, when someone or something has value as an *end* in itself, for its own sake, it has intrinsic value. (A variant of the latter is **inherent value**, meaning that in order to exist, intrinsic value requires at least one or more valuers.[1])

There has been a great deal of confusion around this issue. Let us briefly try to clear it up, if we can. In the first place, the distinction between instrumental and intrinsic value is necessary. Why? Because each such term depends for its meaning on the contrasting one it is defined against. Furthermore, if there were only instrumental value, then *everything* would only have value as a means to something else; but for something to have value as a means, that something else must, at least in practice and relative to the means, have value in itself. In other words, it must have intrinsic value. But if there was only intrinsic value, it is not at all clear how it would actually be possible to live, i.e., without using anything or anyone.

Second – and this confusion relates closely to the subject of the earlier discussion of realism and relativism – there is the vexed question (among environmental philosophers) of whether intrinsic value is 'objective' or 'subjective'. Much ink has been spilled in debates between realists or objectivists, who assert that value is 'really there', 'actually there' or even 'out there', and relativists or subjectivists, who argue that we 'project', 'create' or 'construct' it. The former use their assertion to argue for the pre-eminence of science among all the ways of knowing. For their part, the subjectivists, who also believe that there is such a thing as True Knowledge but that we cannot have it, hold that any agreement is therefore arbitrary.

The problem is that both sides, or rather dogmatic proponents of both these views, tend to talk past each other. The resulting stalemate is unnecessary, however, for the same sort of reasons mentioned earlier in the section on epistemology.[2] On the one hand, there can be no value that is objective *in the sense of* being 'out there' whether we know it or not. Any such value (like anything else) has no reality, let alone meaning, for us; to put it bluntly, reality just *is* reality-for-us (whoever 'us' might be – it certainly need not be just human).

On the other hand, neither is value created willy-nilly, conjured by us out of nothing, and as whatever we wish. So nor is it subjective *in the sense of* being purely our personal creation; we only exist in, and not apart from, a world of others which exercises constant constraints.

We should therefore abandon the untenably extreme views according to which value must either be completely independent of human apprehension, in order to qualify as objective, or else 'merely' subjective, meaning arbitrary or trivial, and therefore (in another variation) in need of some kind of other support, usually scientific.[3] This is a false choice. Value requires both a world *and* participation by valuers to be real. It is both objective – 'really there . . .' – *and* subjective: '. . . for us'.

In short, whatever has intrinsic value is *whatever is valued for its own sake*, without any reference to its usefulness in realizing some other goal. Now it may be too strong to maintain, with John Fowles, that 'We shall never understand nature (or ourselves), and certainly never respect it, until we dissociate the wild from the notion of usability – however innocent or harmless the use' (1979: 43–4). But there are certainly good grounds for holding that nature must not be seen as *only* of instrumental value.

With this in mind, we can turn to the next major distinction: between anthropocentrism, which limits most if not all intrinsic value to humans, and ecocentrism, which finds intrinsic value in nature. (In practice that can mean non-human nature, but properly speaking, as we shall see, it should include humans.)

## Anthropocentrism

Anthropocentrism – literally, human-centredness – is one of the most contentious ideas, and therefore words, in ecological ethics. There have been several attempts to replace it but none has been particularly convincing, and since some such concept is definitely needed, it would probably be better to stick with this one while being careful about exactly what we mean by it.

One objection to the term can be cleared up right away. It goes something like this: 'For us, everything is necessarily human-centred. Therefore there is no alternative, and the term is meaningless.' This point (already overstretched) is then used to argue that all value is human, and that ethics should therefore have human beings as its principal or even sole focus: ' "Man" never left centre stage, nature *never has been, and never will be*, recognized as autonomous' (Jordanova 1987).[4]

The premise here is perfectly true. All value, for us, is *anthropogenic*: generated by human experience (although always co-created with, and in, worlds). But because value is generated *by* human beings, it does not follow that humans must be the main repository or central concern *of* value. Similarly, recognition of the intrinsic value of the natural world may require a human valuer. (Although, are we the only animals to value it? I doubt it!) Again, it does not follow that such value is therefore *itself* purely human. As David Wiggins put it, 'In thinking about ecological things we ought not to pretend (and we do not need to pretend) that we have any alternative, as human beings, but to bring to bear upon ecological questions the human scale of values. . . . [But] The human scale of values is by no means exclusively a scale of human values' (2000: 7–8).[5]

Notwithstanding these points, however, there are those who maintain that as a matter of existential or metaphysical fact, humanity is the principal or sole thing of value, and that the only appropriate or possible scale of value for humans is a scale of human values. We therefore still need a word signifying this position. Now, the use of 'anthropocentrism' has been criticized, not without reason, as too sweeping. After all, there is nothing wrong with a concern for human beings as such, nor is it necessarily inconsistent with a concern for non-human nature.[6] For this reason, alternative terms have been suggested such as *human chauvinism*, *speciesism* and *human racism*.[7] These all have some merit, although the first term is awkward, the second a clumsy neologism, and the third involves too narrow an analogy. More important still, however, by now the term 'anthropocentrism' is pretty well established. Also, there is already a reasonably good word for a healthy and non-exclusive appreciation of human value, namely *humanism* (although for the story of its modern corruption, see Ehrenfeld's (1981) excellent analysis). For these reasons, I think we should retain 'anthropocentrism' to refer to *the unjustified privileging of human beings, as such, at the expense of other forms of life* (analogous to such prejudices as racism or sexism).

It is vital to recognize how dominant this mindset is, whether in politics, economics, science or culture. Neil Evernden, in *The Natural Alien*, calls it 'resourcism': 'a kind of modern religion

which casts all of creation into categories of utility' to humans,
whereby there is literally nothing in the natural (and human) world
which cannot be 'transformed into a resource' (1985: 23). It is the
ideology *par excellence* of modernity, and thus of ecocrisis.[8] And its
expression vis-à-vis the natural world is in various forms of *managerial environmentalism*.[9]

## Ecocentrism

Here we come to the opposite position, and it is very important
one, both in itself and as a counterpole to anthropocentrism. There
are intermediate positions, of course. One is (let us say) *zoocentrism*, according to which the principal locus of value is animals (in
practice, non-human animals).[10] Another, less limited and arbitrary,
is *biocentrism*: life itself as value, in all its forms (organisms). So why
is this an intermediate position? Because, simply put, life is itself
dependent on components aptly summarized in the ancient elements: earth, air, water and fire (sunlight). Ecosystems thus comprise a complex ongoing dance of interrelationships not only
with other organisms but with the non-organic. For this reason,
*ecocentrism* is the more inclusive concept – and value.[11]

Not surprisingly, ecocentrism is at least equally as contentious
and delicate a matter as anthropocentrism. At first sight, it seems,
its meaning should be simple: placing, or finding, value in the
natural world.[12] But the crucial question is, does, or should, that
include human beings? Critics of ecocentrism have charged it with
a simple inversion of anthropocentrism which is not only misanthropic (and strategically counterproductive) but preserves the
radical split between the human and natural worlds that we inherited from Platonism, Christianity and Cartesianism. That split is one
which ecologists in general see as an integral part of the problem.
And the accusation of misanthropy is not always without
justification, where some populist Deep Ecologists are concerned.

But there is no reason why compassion for human beings and
compassion for non-human animals and nature should have to be
mutually exclusive. Logically speaking, if humans are a part of

nature, then they share, at least in part and/or potentially, in nature's intrinsic value. And in practice, the two kinds of compassion are likely to *reinforce* each other. (It is also significant that those who are cruel to animals are more likely to abuse other people and vice versa.) Ecocentrism does not necessarily exclude humanity, and there are powerful reasons – strategic as well as ethical – why it should not. Warwick Fox is right that 'being opposed to human-centredness is logically distinct from being opposed to humans per se' (1995: 19). And misanthropy is as unjustifiable as it is unattractive. As Robyn Eckersley writes, respecting the Earth's bounty, 'The principle of common entitlement makes it clear that humans are not expected to subvert their own *basic* needs in order to enable other life-forms to flourish' (1998: 177).

Humanity poses a conundrum in this respect, being plainly *part* of the natural world and, at the same time, *distinct* from other animals in the degree to which individual reflective consciousness, and its socialization as culture, affects to a relatively unique extent how otherwise 'purely' natural factors play themselves out. Note that no superiority or special privileges necessarily follow from this uniqueness.[13] But it does mean that ethically, as Ken Jones puts it, in an excellent discussion, 'Humankind does have a unique responsibility for the wellbeing of other creatures and the whole ecosystem, yet is at the same time a dependent and integral part of that system' (1993: 97). So neither exclusive anthropocentrism nor exclusive ecocentrism is a defensible, or desirable, option.

However, it is vital to recognize that even with an inclusive ecocentrism, there can be serious conflicts between humans and non-human nature; and an arrangement in which the former *cannot lose*, if and when there are such conflicts, cannot be called ecocentric. Some people – social ecologists, for example – maintain that the 'liberation' of nature (a rather anthropocentric and patronizing idea in any case) *necessarily* follows from the liberation of oppressed humans.[14] But this wishful thinking obscures the real conflicts and hard choices that can occur between what are at least perceived as humans' and nature's interests, and makes it harder to evaluate and decide between them. There are many possible examples: should DDT be banned on ecological grounds, even though that would jeopardize the eradication of malaria in the Third World? In a world of rapidly shrinking wild enclaves and widespread species decline, should aboriginal people be permitted to hunt and trap within the few remaining protected areas? Indeed, even within the broad movement to protect the non-human world, there are clashes between proponents of animal liberation/rights (trying to protect individual animals) and ecologists/environmentalists (trying to protect species and/or ecosystems).[15] Alliances between different progressive and emancipatory movements do not come ready-made; the hard work of forging them is unavoidable. And it should be added that in many, perhaps even most, situations, an appeal to anthropocentric value (human self-interest) may be an unavoidable part of the argument for an ecocentric outcome.

It follows that an ecocentric ethic alone will probably not suffice to save an Earth fit for life as we know it; but that also won't happen without one. In our unprecedented circumstances, the dominant philosophy of the last two millennia (either in religious or secular form) is now in drastic need of change. Ecocentrism recognizes, as anthropocentrism does not, that human beings live in a *more-than-human world*, of which they are only one part.[16]

Anthropocentrism's denial of such a fundamental point cannot be corrected by 'enlightened self-interest', through limited add-ons. The latter cannot place the perception of uselessness *to us* (especially economically) in the contexts which draw its poison: the extraordinary complexity of the natural world on the one hand, and the extent of our ignorance and our greed on the other.[17] The problem with 'enlightened anthropocentrism' is exactly the same as with 'enlightened egoism'; as Midgley says, 'egoism is by its nature rather *un*enlightened and hard to enlighten' (1997: 94). The important thing now, as Sylvan and Bennett write, is to 'set anthropocentric concerns within ecocentric concerns' (1994: 90).

At the moment, of course, just the opposite is almost universally the case, and the results, jeopardizing both humanity and non-human nature, are all too evident. An ecocentric 'horizon' to our concerns, in contrast, would help avert ecological disaster, and do so in a way that also furthers anthropocentric interests: 'if humans do learn to care about what happens to other species and ecosystems – that is, to treat nature as if it mattered – then the repercussions [of ecological destruction] to humans will be lessened' (ibid. 6).

# 6

## Light Green or Shallow (Anthropocentric) Ethics

We have now arrived, via value, at ecological ethics as such: that is, principles (incorporating values) concerning how human beings ought to behave in relation to non-human nature. Here, too, there is a spectrum. At one end, corresponding to instrumental value, consideration for the non-human is only indirect, insofar as the well-being of humans is affected. In the middle, there is consideration for non-human individuals. At the other end, corresponding to intrinsic value, we find consideration for the well-being of non-human places and ecosystems. We shall consider several different kinds of each of these three principal positions, especially the last.[1]

### What is a Light Green Ethic?

Its chief characteristic is that of limiting direct value to human beings. In other words, it is anthropocentric. Non-human beings of any kind have no independent moral status or considerability, and only merit consideration insofar as they matter to humans; consequently, any parts of non-human nature that have no use-value for humans are fair game, so to speak, and any parts which apparently have no value can be disposed of. Conversely, an ecological problem is defined here as one that poses difficulties for humans, regardless of its effects on the rest of nature.

I am not assuming that an ecologically sound programme based on light green ethics is impossible. But it would have to include, for example:

- a very strong *precautionary principle* – that is, acting cautiously, on the assumption that our knowledge of the effects of our actions is always exceeded by our ignorance;
- a definition of 'sustainability' that rules out all practices except those that are *indefinitely* sustainable; and, similarly,
- a conviction that as much rather than as little as possible of nature should be preserved intact.

The result, in effect, would favour the survival and possibly flourishing of non-human nature, even if the reason was still human survival and flourishing, and that (from a consequentialist point of view, which in this case seems desirable) would be fine.[2]

The unlikeliness of this degree of enlightened self-interest, on any appreciable scale, should be virtually self-evident. However – given that the well-being of human beings is so intimately tied to the well-being of the natural world – a great deal of ecologically sound regulation and legislation can be defended in terms of human interests. That probably includes almost anything within the current range of political possibility.[3] The problem, however, lies with the serious limitations of human beings when it comes to *perceiving*, let alone acting on, that intimacy. Both individually and collectively, we tend to self-interest narrowly construed, in such a way and to such an extent that our dependence on the natural world is very difficult to notice; and that weakness is literally capitalized on by those with the equally narrow but powerful motive of profit. Many would argue that this existential fact makes an ecocentric ethic unrealistic or even impossible. Another possible conclusion, however, is that it makes one even more necessary and urgent.

In any case, light green or shallow ethics and its accompanying *ethos* (way of behaving) does not even attempt to break out of anthropocentrism. Not surprisingly, this least ecological ethic is also the ruling one. Its roots lie in the dominion thesis discussed earlier, but now secularized. This is the dominant philosophy, where nature is concerned, in government departments and ministries, corporations, research laboratories and institutes of all kinds. Its followers see non-human nature as a resource to be exploited for human ends, and that view is encapsulated in resource management and conservation, human welfare ecology, and a great deal of what is called environmentalism. A light green ethic doesn't preclude precautionary arguments, but its concern is still human well-being. The furthest it can reach in an ecological direction without becoming something else is 'sustainability', which asks, 'How long can we continue to exploit this natural resource without destroying it altogether, and thus not be able to exploit it any longer?' 'Sustainable development' and (still more so) 'sustainable growth', as ecological gestures, are even more transparent; given that nothing is sustainable without limits, which are just what development and growth resist recognizing, these terms translate as: 'How can we have our anthropocentric cake and eat it ecologically?' As Rudolf Bahro pointedly observed, 'Almost everywhere in the world people still want a megamachine which nevertheless doesn't destroy anything, and they don't want to know they can't have one' (1994: 56).[4]

The light green view has recently found new and more sophisticated expression among techno-optimists, who use the ever-increasing impact of humans on global ecosystems to advocate more of the same: what the late Stan Rowe (1995) called 'managing profligacy more efficiently', or what amounts to a more scientific plundering of 'resources' and further attempted evasion of natural limits on human desires.[5] A related project is to put a price on (potentially) everything, thus allowing ecological 'costing'.[6] The anthropocentric bias of this effort, as well as its potential ruthlessness, is exposed by the fact that while there is some recognition of the abuse of nature by humans as well as its use, there is none for its *non*-use. The title of a book by James Trefil says it all: *Human Nature: A Blueprint for Managing the Earth − by People, for People* (2004).

The ultimate expression of this philosophy is the idea that, having done such a good job of managing itself and the world to date, the duty of humanity is now to take charge of evolution and, principally through genetic engineering, direct it: a kind of 'intelligent species' burden', as Fox aptly puts it (1995: 195).[7] The fine print specifies that it is, of course, scientists (the brain of collective humanity, perhaps?) whom we are to allow to lead, and to morally, politically and financially support, in this adventure.[8]

Such advocacy, common among sociobiologists and evolutionary psychologists, is often identified as politically right-wing. If so, then it is ironic to consider for a moment a movement which characterizes itself as on the left (albeit anarchist rather than socialist): *social ecology*.[9] In this view, human–nature relations depend completely upon human–human relations, so that improving the former depends entirely on resolving the latter; any serious ethical consideration of non-human nature is therefore superceded by intrahuman politics. Furthermore, in its founder Murray Bookchin's words, it is 'the responsibility of the most conscious life-form – humanity – to be the "voice" of a mute nature' (ibid. 44).[10] This seems patronizing at best, and at worst an invitation to the kind of self-serving anthropocentrism and utilitarianism we have just been discussing. Bookchin's advocacy of evolutionary stewardship could legitimate the wildest current aspirations of biotechnology. At their best, social ecologists perform valuable political and social service, both theoretical and practical, in the form of municipal and community development; but these, while valuable in themselves, leave the heart of the ecological crisis untouched.

Such agreement across the usual political spectrum is instructive. It reveals that the differences between such political opponents are frequently not, at least in this context, fundamental; both subscribe to a shallow ecological ethic.

Note, however, that the very dominance of this ethic – not only among those in positions of authority, but also among members of the public – means that in many actual situations, a direct connection to human interests may be the only *available* argument for ecologists to fall back on. And it may well serve for a while, or in an immediate crisis, as long as a human use-value for the natural item (plant or animal, species or place) can be found. It may even be possible to stretch the concept of 'use' beyond its normal boundaries: for example, to argue that an item's use is that it meets our aesthetic or spiritual needs. Ultimately, though, for the reasons I have mentioned, shallow ecological ethics as a way to defend nature is inadequate.

Another and more disturbing irony is that even much so-called environmentalism falls into this category. Why disturbing? Because, as a few lone voices have pointed out, with 'resourcism' the terms of the debate are already loaded in favour of human interests, themselves almost always construed in narrow and relatively immediate economic terms:

> The basic attitude towards the non-human has not even been challenged in the rush to embrace utilitarian conservation. By basing all arguments on enlightened self-interest the environmentalists have ensured their own failure whenever self-interest can be perceived as lying elsewhere. . . . The industrialist and the environmentalist are brothers under the skin; they differ merely as to the best use the natural world ought to be put to. (Evernden 1985: 10)[11]

In theory, then, anthropocentric ethics alone could perhaps suffice to restore sanity to humanity's relationships with the rest of the natural world, *if* it were sufficiently enlightened; and, in practice, it can sometimes take us part of the way. But the rub is in that 'if'. The evidence that self-interest can ever be that enlightened, on sufficiently widespread, deep and long-lasting a scale, is vanishingly small. Facing up to that uncomfortable fact obliges us to recognize that, ecologically speaking, 'enlightened self-interest' is ultimately an oxymoron.

Incidentally, there is an interesting paradox at work in light green ethics. Anthropocentric apologists for human superiority frequently argue that (in the words of one defender of animal experiments), 'All animals put their own survival first, and we should do the same'.[12] This attitude assumes a human nature that is ethically *identical* with that of other animals; the only difference lies in our superior power, resulting from the contingent success of our evolutionary position. Political ecologists, on the other hand – by which I mean those who are not only aware of the ecosystemic natural world but who value its integrity – argue that human beings can, and should, choose not to exploit our species dominance by expanding in every way possible. This assumes that we are significantly *different* from all other animals, which are presumably incapable of practising quasi-voluntary restraint (and probably do not need to).

The question for the latter group then becomes, how can you argue for ecocentrism without thereby encouraging human exceptionalism? The answer is, you can't, and that is all right – as long as difference does not slip into superiority, and our participation in and dependence upon nature is given its due weight. (The capacity to be moral is not, as such, a sign of superiority, and any privilege it entails would seem to be a demanding one of care, service and even sacrifice.)

## Lifeboat Ethics

I would like to turn now to a particular kind of shallow ethics known as 'lifeboat ethics'. Its originator, the late Garrett Hardin, pointed out that natural resources are necessarily limited, and that the human population is now well past what those resources can support without measures, such as the 'Green Revolution' and now biotechnology, which will simply result in further population increases, and thus more strain on resources, etc. (For criticizing these, he has widely been accused of callousness.) He therefore suggested that the most appropriate metaphor for the situation facing humanity is that of a lifeboat: the wealthier societies live in a relatively (but *not*, note, infinitely) capacious boat, with room for some but certainly not all of the remaining (and more numerous) human flotsam in the sea. The most just solution, to pick them all up, would simply sink the boat. The only real questions, then, are how many and who to allow on board?

This metaphor captures some of the dilemmas which some people and their societies face, and to accuse Hardin of cruelty is simply to shoot the messenger. A lifeboat ethic is applicable to situations, which do sometimes occur, where there are no good ethical solutions, only a choice, initially, of whether to choose between various horrors or refuse to do so. Assuming the first course is taken, one can only hope further choices are less evil than the alternatives. (This is similar but not quite identical with triage, where there is a more-or-less rational set of criteria for determining which two, of any three, should be saved.)

A more serious limitation of lifeboat ethics, in an ecological context, is that if, as Mary Midgley has remarked, it is actually the *human* lifeboat that is sinking, it doesn't make much sense to respond, 'Not at my end!' (1997: 93). True, the poor and defenceless will be hit hardest, but if the scale of the crisis is sufficiently serious, ultimately no one will be exempt.

Another influential metaphor of Hardin's is **the tragedy of the commons** (1968). In this view, briefly, any common good that is communally owned invites abuse by free-riders taking advantage of unlimited access; combined with its limited resources, this will result in its destruction. His argument has been widely interpreted as a right-wing one for privatization as the best way to protect nature, but Hardin himself was not so simple-minded. Pointing out that limited resources cannot meet unlimited demands, and in a commons, freedom (a frequent right-wing libertarian byword) therefore brings ruin to all, he called for 'mutual coercion, mutually agreed upon by the majority of the people affected' – which is not a bad description of, simply, regulation.

The problem with Hardin's idea is that it assumes a capitalist kind of common, which approaches a contradiction in terms. Or rather, the commons it describes – and for which one could justifiably also use the term 'community' – is one in which custom has *already* broken down; and historically, overwhelmingly, that has happened under the impact of capitalism, allied with imperialism.[13] As E. P. Thompson wrote of Hardin's theory, 'Despite its commonsense air, what it overlooks is that the commoners themselves were not without commonsense. Over time and over space the users of commons have developed a rich variety of institutions and community sanctions which have effected restraints and stints upon use' (1991).[14] Hardin's criticism is therefore not really so much of commons as of capitalism, or rather the kind of commons, in such respects as scale and organization, that results from capitalism.[15]

As Kohak recognizes, 'Hardin's greatest and most unpopular contribution may be his willingness to face the reality that some solution must be found even when none is acceptable. . . . Our possibilities are limited, our demands unlimited: if we are to survive, we must limit them ourselves' (2000: 96–7). And although his work remains within anthropocentric light green ethics – it is only concerned with the fate of humans – this insight transcends that boundary.

# 7

## Mid-Green or Intermediate Ethics

In Sylvan and Bennett's terms, intermediate ethics denies the Sole Value Assumption – that humans alone have any intrinsic value – but subscribes to a modified version, the Greater Value Assumption, according to which natural items have some intrinsic value, but wherever they conflict with human interests the latter must take precedence. (There is, however, a range of opinion regarding whether those interests must be 'vital' ones, and what exactly constitutes them.) It follows that here, ecological problems are not defined solely in terms of problems they cause to humans; but there are sharp limits to this advance. Wilderness preservation, for example, is defensible in these terms as the preservation of something which does indeed have some intrinsic value which also meets some human (aesthetic, etc.) needs; where oil, minerals and other apparently vital needs are concerned, however, the former must give way.

The other way of defining mid-range ecological ethics (which is not necessarily consistent with the first) is as non-anthropocentric but not fully ecocentric. That is, value is not restricted to human beings, but it also does not extend all the way to ecosystems. As we shall see, this is the position of biocentrism. Its main way of proceeding is to build on anthropocentrism by arguing that what has been thought of as a solely human value is also true of non-humans.

Called *moral extensionism*, it extends moral considerability to (primarily) other animals, which are therefore perceived as possessing independent moral status, and therefore as deserving protection for their own sakes, regardless of whether they matter to human beings.

Some defenders of human chauvinism (e.g., Passmore 1974) have argued that qualification for such membership depends on also being a moral agent. But if so, as Midgley (1992) has pointed out, one would also have to exclude from ethical consideration children, the senile, the temporarily and the permanently insane, defectives, embryos (human and otherwise), sentient animals, non-sentient animals, plants, artefacts (including art), inanimate objects, groups of all kinds, ecosystems, landscapes and places, countries, the biosphere and potentially oneself – in other words, the majority of entities with whom we have to deal.[1]

Extensionism remains human-centred, however; it retains the assumption that humans come with deontological 'rights' which can in certain cases be extended to honorary humans, but which otherwise trump all other considerations. Such a position is vulnerable to 'rights' that have been transmogrified into straightforwardly non-vital wants, usually with the help of an economic system whose considerable resources are dedicated to creating and exploiting just that process.

This kind of ethics can best be considered in terms of its leading schools, as follows.

## Animal Liberation

The movement that bears its name began with the book *Animal Liberation* (1977) by Peter Singer, mentioned above in the earlier section on utilitarianism. Using as a starting point Bentham's famous rhetorical question quoted there, Singer has bravely tackled the horrendous suffering, and sheer scale of that suffering, we inflict on other animals. In the USA *alone*, about 70 *million* animals are annually used in medical and pharmaceutical experiments, and 5 *billion* live and die in so-called factory farms.[2]

This is the moral basis of the case for vegetarianism – or, at least, for not eating factory-farmed animals and for working towards banning animal experiments. Taking these in reverse order, the latter question is, of course, a kind of litmus test for where anthropocentrism ends and mid-green ethics begins. A compromise might be possible along these lines: 'I only support medical experiments on animals where nothing less than human lives are at stake and there is no known substitute for such experiments, and I shall encourage the development of other procedures as fully and as quickly as possible.' That position would seem defensible to most people, but it is certainly not ethically impregnable. A fully mid-green commitment would deem it a fudge, as is evident from the words of Rudolf Bahro, a founding member of the German Green Party, when he resigned after it voted to approve animal experiments:

> Yesterday, on the subject of animal experiments, it clearly came down in favour of the position taken by the speaker who said: 'If even one human life can be saved, the torture of animals is permissible.' This sentence expresses the basic principle by which human beings are exterminating plants, animals, and finally themselves. (1986: 210)

Turning to the question of diet, the amount of suffering that humans in the developed world now inflict upon other animals could be greatly lessened if, at the very *least*, (1) their welfare were taken seriously and (2) meat was removed from the category of cheap fast food. If one 'must' eat meat, then one has a clear-cut ethical responsibility to ensure that the animal lives well while it lives, and doesn't die for any trivial reason such as 'I fancy a hamburger'. The cheapness of meat does not justify its consumption; there are other kinds of food that could be offered as inexpensively and much more nutritiously. It is the meat industry, not the poor, that benefits from the current situation.[3] Meat consumed infrequently, perhaps only on special occasions, and preferably with some knowledge of what that animal's sacrifice actually involved (which should be an educational requirement), would go a long way to realizing that goal. Full vegetarianism, the next step, requires the additional point – which certainly seems highly plausible – that it is quite simply wrong to kill animals that have as much interest in staying alive as we do (and make that interest quite plain when they come to be killed) for our non-essential desires.[4] Note that this position does not rule out eating meat when there is no other option to survive.

The same general case can be made on other grounds. A typical Western diet, for example, uses more than four times more land than is needed for a vegetarian diet, and farmed animals consume a third of the world's total cereal production, along with a great deal of its precious drinking water, while producing trillions of tons of untreated waste.[5] (Note that these problems can be seen as either anthropocentric – if addressed, more humans could live better lives – or ecocentric – there would be less suffering, less pollution and more room, food and water for other life-forms and ecosystems; or both.)

Of course, industrial husbandry is part of a millennium-long history of brutality (an ironic term in this context) on the part of humans towards their fellow animals, including the slaughter of wild animals. Coleman (2004) for example, recounts how wolves in North America in the past centuries were not just killed but tortured with deliberate and extravagent cruelty; he asks (but cannot really answer) why death was not enough. This is not an isolated example: it is a typical one, and there are certainly grounds for arguing that 'genocide' and even 'holocaust' are concepts that are as appropriate for describing what we have done and are doing to other animals as they are for what we have done and do to each other.[6]

Carried forward by various campaigning organizations, Singer's arguments have already had a significant effect on animal welfare, if still regrettably small in relation to the problem. They have gone far in establishing the ethical point that the literally vital interests of non-human beings should not be violated for relatively trivial human reasons. The key to this advance is *sentience* – especially the ability to *suffer* – together with basic logical consistency. Since we grant moral considerability on that basis to young children and mentally handicapped adults – rather than requiring, say, the ability to reason – it is fundamentally inconsistent to deny it to non-human animals that (or, we should say, who)[7] are also clearly sentient: pigs, chickens, monkeys, sheep, etc., not to mention 'charismatic megafauna' in the wild. The only justification for doing so is therefore what Singer calls **speciesism**: 'a prejudice or attitude of bias in favour of the interests of members of one's own species and against those of members of other species' (1977: 26).[8] Not many people would openly admit to such prejudice, although more, perhaps, than would to racism or sexism. The potential for shaming bad practice – especially when it threatens to erupt in bad corporate publicity – is thus significant. And there are other advantages; one is that there are simple things one can do (such as buy free-range eggs instead of factory-farmed ones). Another is that, as Sylvan and Bennett remark, 'It is easier to empathise with the deer in the field, than the field the deer is in' (1994: 85).

However, as they also point out, this is also the animal liberation movement's weakness: Singer has 'traded human chauvinism for *sentient* chauvinism' (ibid. 87). That is, only sentient beings are deemed worthy of ethical consideration; living but non-sentient ones, such as (so far as we know) plants – let alone ecosystems – are not. The criterion is thus seriously impoverished, and the programme based on it, stopping well short of ecocentrism, cannot protect anything apparently non-sentient. For that, it has to fall back on the relatively weak shallow argument that rainforests (say) should be protected because they are of use to people and animals.

Closely related to the problem with sentience, and equally serious, is Singer's irreducible *individualism*, which means that only individual animals deserve direct moral consideration. Once again, collectivities of any sort are left dangerously exposed. Of course, it would be possible to get from individual animals to collections of them, and even ecosystems, if it was admitted that the welfare of individual wild animals required others of its kind, and other inter-related kinds, flourishing in an undamaged environment. There is little evidence, however, of mid-green animal liberationists being willing or able to take this further step. (And to be fair, they have their hands more than full with what they have set themselves to do.)

## Animal Rights

Also influential is the animals **rights** movement inspired by Tom Regan (1983). Although both its ultimate concerns and its practical

upshot are much the same as that of animal liberation – which therefore need not be repeated – its philosophical basis is different.
Recalling the different emphases of utilitarian and deontological
ethics earlier, Regan bases his programme squarely on human individual rights extended to animals. He argues that all adult mammals,
at least, are self-aware. As 'subjects-of-a-life' (i.e., their own), they
therefore have a *right* to life.

Again, as with Singer, we are compelled to grant that right,
almost universally recognized for humans, to other mammals, on
pain of either inconsistency or ugly and irrational prejudice. Regan
can thus take advantage of modern Western (and especially
American) 'rights culture' to alleviate the suffering of animals. Yet
the animal rights approach shares the same weaknesses, just noted,
as animal liberation. Only individual animals – and 'higher' ones at
that – are granted direct moral considerability. As Holmes Rolston
rightly says, 'Every organism has a good-of-its-kind; it defends its
own kind as a good kind' (1988: 105). In that case, ethical argument
does not begin or end with self-awareness.

In short, the intermediate ethics of both Singer and Regan have
succeeded in extending ethical consideration to (some) animals
only by using a criterion that excludes most of the natural world 'as
surely as the most narrowly human speciesism' (Benson 2000: 87).
The point made by John Rodman in 1977 still stands: 'I need only
to stand in the midst of a clear-cut forest, a strip-mined hillside, a
defoliated jungle, or a dammed canyon to feel uneasy with assumptions that could yield the conclusion that no human action can
make any difference to the welfare of anything but sentient animals'
(1977: 89; quoted in Benson 2000: 87).

## Biocentrism

In ecological ethics, biocentrism – literally, life-centredness – is
associated almost entirely with the work of Paul Taylor and his book
*Respect for Nature*. The central focus here is on what Taylor calls 'an
attitude of respect for nature'. To have this attitude, he writes, 'is to
regard the wild plants and animals of the Earth's natural ecosystems

as possessing inherent worth. That such creatures have inherent worth may be considered the fundamental value presupposition of the attitude of respect' (1986: 71). And in order to possess inherent worth, a being only has to have 'a good of its own', that is to say, it can be benefited or harmed in relation to its potential biological development (ibid. 199). (Sentience, self-consciousness or conscious interest are therefore not required for moral considerability.)

There are four related aspects to this biocentric outlook:

1  Humans are members of the community of life in the same sense, and on the same terms as, other living things.
2  That community, of which humans are a part, consists of a system of interdependence comprising not only physical conditions, but also relations with other members.
3  Every such organism is a teleological centre of life, i.e., an individual pursuing its own kind of good (Greek *telos* = goal or end).
4  Humans are not inherently superior to other organisms. (Ibid. 99ff.)

From these points, Taylor infers that respect should be accorded to *all* organisms, human or otherwise, alike: that is, *unconditionally*. Furthermore, since the flourishing of each is a good thing, it should be promoted; in other words, that is its right and our duty. Finally, since this result applies *universally* (i.e., in theory, without exception), it is a rational 'foundation' for the biocentric position – by implication, the only kind of foundation worth having – and, as such, merits (without any other substantive reasons) the support of all *rational* beings.

Such reasoning and its implicit values, together with the firm emphasis on rights and duties, ought to remind the reader of the earlier section on deontological ethics. Although Taylor extends Kant's human-centred system to other animals and into the arena of mid-green ethics, which is a definite advance, his work – like that of the arch-Kantian John Rawls – suffers from an arcane and impractical rationalism, which is therefore unlikely to leave much of a mark outside the intellectual and legal academy. (This, of course, is a broadly consequentialist criticism.)

The other problem with biocentrism is its individualism. Like other kinds of mid-green or intermediate ethics, Taylor's 'respect for nature' is indeed non-anthropocentric, but it really denotes respect for life, that is, *individual living things*. Such an ethic cannot handle a non-random collection of individuals such as a species, and the challenge of the point made by Rolston that 'Every extinction is a kind of super-killing. . . . It kills birth as well as death' (1992: 141). Nor can it directly address – as our current ecocrisis urgently requires – the non-random collection of individuals that is an embedded ecological community (or series of overlapping communities). But these points have already been discussed as limitations of a deontological ethics, so now let us turn to ethics which does recognize such 'things' as fully deserving of direct moral consideration.

# 8

## Dark Green or Deep (Ecocentric) Ethics

### A Suggested Definition

Ecocentric (literally, Earth-centred) ethics, like biocentrism, is non-anthropocentric. However, they differ in that ecocentric or dark green ethics takes as objects of ethical concern **holistic** entities (although that can and usually does include individuals); and those entities include integral components that are non-living as well as animate.

An ecocentric, dark green or deep ecological ethics, I suggest, must be able to satisfy at least these criteria:

1  *It must be able to recognize the value, and therefore support the ethical defence, of the integrity of species and of ecosystemic places, as well as human and non-human organisms.* So it is holistic, although not in the sense of necessarily excluding considerations of individual value.
2  Within nature-as-value, it must (a) *allow for conflicts between the interests of human and non-human nature*; (b) *allow human interests, on occasion, to lose.* (It is hardly a level playing-field otherwise.)

Thus, dark green ethics rejects both the Sole and the Greater Value Assumptions in favour of the idea that some or all natural beings, in the broadest sense, have independent moral status.[1] Ecological problems are not solely defined by reference to human beings (although they can be so defined), other natural entities deserve protection regardless of their use or value to humans, and nature has intrinsic value (although there is room for differences about exactly what that means) which may, in specific instances, predominate over human value. In one way or another, all dark green schools subscribe to the position that 'the ecological community forms the ethical community' (Sylvan and Bennett 1994: 91), and although we shall look at Sylvan's Deep-Green Theory separately later on, it is fair to borrow his description of it for ecocentric ethics as such: they 'find all standard ethics mired in heavy prejudice, a prejudice in favour of things human and against things non-human' (ibid. 139–40).

Of the several possible objections to this definition, let me briefly address two. One is that the concept of ecological integrity (or a natural or healthy condition) is now considered to be more complex and contingent than when it was assumed that every ecosystem naturally arrived at a 'climax state'. That is true, but it does not invalidate the sense of integrity 'in terms of the capacity of the Earth's ecosystems to continue functioning so that the environmental services are maintained upon which the wellbeing of humans and all life depend' (Mackey 2004: 79).[2] (Note, however, the inaptness of the term 'environmental services' when what is serving and what is being served are, in actuality, inseparable; and the danger of a narrow definition of 'well-being' by those for whom a broad one would be inconvenient.)

The second possible objection can be disposed of quickly: 'Who sides with non-human nature if not people? So how can an ethic be ecocentric?' Of course this is an ethic *for* humans; but that does not mean humans can or must side only *with* humans. (The parallel with the confusion between anthropogenic and anthropocentric is precise.)

Ecocentric ethics is our principal concern in this book. The urgency of its contemporary relevance seems matched only by the extent to which it has been ignored or disparaged. For this reason, let us now turn, in more detail and depth, to the principal varieties of ecocentrism.[3]

# The Land Ethic

The Land Ethic was formulated by the wildlife biologist and conservationist Aldo Leopold (1887–1948) in *A Sand County Almanac with Essays on Conservation from Round River* (1948). More a work of mature reflection than academic philosophy, this became perhaps the single most influential statement (and certainly so in America) of ecocentric ethics. That has been assisted by its further development by J. Baird Callicott (1987, 1989).

A number of Leopold's pithier maxims have, with good reason, taken firm root in green ethical discourse. Let us review them, with some comments. One is that '*A thing is right when it tends to preserve the integrity, stability and beauty of the biotic community. It is wrong when it tends otherwise*' (1970: 262). The 'biotic community' is potentially misleading here; it is not, like biocentrism, limited to biota or organisms. As Leopold also wrote, 'The land ethic simply enlarges the boundaries of the community to include soils, waters, plants, and animals, or collectively: the land' (ibid. 239). (It does not require much of a leap of imagination to extend this idea to include an *ocean ethic*, as of course it should.[4])

The virtues of this formulation are considerable. First, it is fully ethical in the sense of specifying what is good/bad and right/wrong, and (in its intention) consequentially so. As Leopold realized, an essential part of an ethic is limiting what can and cannot be done – in this case, ecologically. Note that a limitation on human freedom is the very thing most often and bitterly rejected by adherents of anthropocentric ethics and instrumental value, for whom nature is (and must be kept as) an ethically inconsiderable resource for humans to do with whatever they wish. Such defensive hostility is a backhanded compliment to the merits of Leopold's suggestion.

Second, its focus is an unambiguously ecocentric one which does not restrict ethical consideration to either the animate (thus excluding ecosystemic places) or individuals (thus excluding wholes and relations). Leopold recognized the Earth itself as possessing 'a certain kind and degree of life' (1991: 95), and infers from his grasp of ecology how it is not only context but creator. Unlike any of the ethics we have so far discussed, the Land Ethic thus qualifies as a dark green or deep one.[5] And, third, its clarity and simplicity are also very helpful in getting the message across – no small matter.

To enlarge the community in such a way does not simply reframe ethical discourse. As Leopold noted, 'a land ethic changes the role of *Homo sapiens* from conquerer of the land-community to *plain member and citizen of it*' (1970: 240; although 'peculiar member' might be more apt). What a radical change that is, or would be.

No ethical position is without its problems, of course. A potentially serious one here arises from Leopold's holism, namely that individual interests could be unduly overridden in the interest of (someone's particular version of) the collective whole; this has invited the somewhat overheated charge of 'environmental fascism' from Tom Regan, the defender of individual animal rights (1984: 362). It is certainly true that there is a clear difference (axiological and ethical) between the emphases of the Land Ethic on the one hand and animal liberation and/or rights on the other.

Indeed, that difference is one reason why the former qualifies as dark green where the latter is not. As Callicott has rightly pointed out, any distinction between 'inner' and 'outer' or 'self' and 'other' is strictly relative and never ultimate, except as a modernist fantasy: 'it is impossible to find a clear demarcation between oneself and one's environment. . . . The world is, indeed, one's extended body' (1989: 113).[6] But such holism is not necessarily collectivist in an authoritarian (let alone fascist) way. As Callicott also suggests, there is nothing in Leopold's work to suggest that the Land Ethic was intended to replace all other ethics; instead, it was to be added to the others, and contextualize them in a new way. A conflict between the ecological good and that of any individual human where the latter must give way can thus not be ruled out (we often have that already, where the common good is restricted to its social version), but it does not follow from the Land Ethic as such.[7]

Another potential problem, more strictly philosophical, is the one discussed earlier of trying to infer an ethical 'ought' from a factual 'is' – in this case, the injunction to value and protect nature from knowledge produced by the science of ecology. And it is true that Leopold often seems to be doing just this. (So too, with less excuse, does Callicott.) But his goal was, and surely ours still is, not the hopeless enterprise of arriving at a philosophically (or, for that matter, scientifically) impeccable theory which will command the assent of all rational beings, etc. Rather, it is to articulate a reasonably coherent, consistent and clear set of ethical principles, informed by and conveying ecocentric values, which will lend themselves to incorporation into people's attitudes and ways of life.

This is a political, social and cultural programme, not a purely logical one. Nor should it try to be all-encompassing, dominating or replacing all other considerations. A normative ecological imperative such as the Land Ethic – or any of the others discussed here – can only hope to acquire sufficient influence in the world to *check* anthropocentrism, instrumentalism and utilitarianism; not to eliminate greed, stupidity and hate in relation to our home and fellow creatures, but to sufficiently reduce their scope.[8]

Who, it might also be objected, is to say what a particular biotic community's 'integrity, beauty and stability' consists of? It is not self-evident, especially given (as earlier mentioned) that contemporary ecological science has changed since Leopold's day and no longer perceives 'climax' states, for example, but more complex successions. But the answer to this fear is implicit in the question. The Land Ethic introduces no new demands or problems here. Decisions about what matters most in any given situation are already taken everywhere, all the time. And such decisions are always axiological and political; they have *never* been purely scientific. Science requires judgement as much as any other human enterprise, and that judgement necessarily involves values, emotions and ideas that have not themselves been arrived at 'scientifically'.[9] We may update Leopold's definition of an ecosystem as 'now meaning something more akin to a locale, [it] has integrity and stability to the degree that it is capable of sustaining biological processes' (Des Jardins 2001: 201) and that is indeed helpful, but such refinements cannot ever relieve us of the responsibility of making ethical decisions on ethical grounds.

It is also to the point that Leopold's own understanding of ecology involved a grasp (unlike so many of the techno-managerial 'ecologists' of today) that the immense complexity of ecosystems is matched by our own relative ignorance. The upshot is the advice, when dealing with the natural world, to proceed with respect, caution and, whenever possible, a light touch – what we earlier identified as the precautionary principle. Working with rather than overruling evolutionary changes, encouraging native species, and preferring biological to artefactual (engineering) solutions would be good examples (ibid. 198). Cross-species gene transfers, before releasing the resulting organisms to interact with those in the wild, would definitely not; nor would 'relocating' habitats.[10]

Such an emphasis is part of what Leopold had in mind when he recommended that we learn to *'think like a mountain'* (1970: 129–33): that is, to see things from (say) a mountain's perspective, with its time-scale and, indeed, priorities. This metaphor has been adopted by Deep Ecologists, who have given it a flavour at once mystical and literal-minded. But they have a point; it is anthropocentrism (especially in its Cartesian modernist form) that has restricted subjectivity and agency to human beings. Indeed, its extreme scientific expression has long been trying to eliminate this last stronghold, in a programme of perfect, if suicidal, consistency. Ecocentrism must counter that attempt with many subjectivities and perspectives, including non-human ones.[11]

## Gaia Theory

Gaia Theory is the name that is replacing its original tag, 'the Gaia Hypothesis'.[12] It was suggested thirty-five years ago, and subsequently developed, primarily by the independent scientist James Lovelock, although Lynn Margulis has also made important contributions.[13] The basic idea is that the Earth is more like a living organism than an inanimate machine, which is made up of highly complex interacting ecosystems binding together not only the continents, oceans and atmosphere, but also its living inhabitants; and like an organism, it is (within limits) self-renewing, adjusting to changing conditions through feedback loops in order to maintain relative stability, especially of the atmosphere and temperature.

Gaia and its inhabitants co-evolve together in a web of relationships of which symbiosis (not, as in most evolutionary theory, competition) is the dominant kind.

'Gaia' is the name of the ancient Greek goddess of the Earth, which Lovelock adopted, following a suggestion by the novelist William Golding. It has aroused a great deal of hostility among scientists who, significantly, seem to feel that animism (the world, and/or its parts, as alive) is still the Enemy; on the other hand, it has also conferred on the theory an accessible and, to others, attractive handle.

The description of the Earth as a super-organism is controversial even among its supporters, some of whom prefer an emphasis on systems theory, with its stress on physical states changing over time, weather patterns, etc.[14] The point is moot, since it could be argued that a sufficiently complex and autonomous 'machine' would eventually become indistinguishable from an 'organism'. But the basic objection seems to be that Gaia Theory merely offers a new (or old) metaphor without specifying any mechanisms. However, the basis of the objection is itself metaphorical, despite assuming its own 'objective' validity: namely the metaphor, beginning in the mid-seventeenth century, of the world and all its parts as a machine.[15]

Gaia Theory started out as a scientific theory but it has had, and will continue to have, a significant impact in other contexts; so it is fair, and indeed important, to ask what kind of *ethics* follows from it.[16] The inclusion of inanimate elements, as integral to animate life – or rather, as at least equally integral to the life of the Earth as its organisms – points toward ecocentrism. So too does the holist emphasis, which is perhaps stronger in this ethic than in any other considered here. But as with the Land Ethic, that emphasis is double-edged. Positively, there are urgent ecological problems which are very hard to bring under the umbrella (so vital in many, even most other, respects) of place, specific ecosystems and localism.[17] Without underestimating the importance of making local and national progress, the issues of fluorocarbons and the ozone layer, and carbon dioxide emissions and global warming, require international scientific cooperation in order to collect and evaluate evidence, and demand international political cooperation for their resolution. They also present a kind of quasi-universal challenge to

much of life as such. Note too the salutary point that humans constitute only one player, albeit currently a major one, in the Gaian
drama; even if we succeed in making the planet uninhabitable for
ourselves, we will undoubtedly be survived by other forms of life,
and by Gaia herself. A likelier scenario is that humanity will survive,
but in extremely difficult circumstances in a biotically degraded and
impoverished world.

Note, however, that in so doing we would take many other forms
of life with us, entirely non-voluntarily, and cause unimaginable
suffering to them as well as to other humans. And nothing in Gaia
Theory actually specifies – as I believe a fully ecocentric theory
should – that this matters ethically. In fact, rather like Hardin's
lifeboat ethics (with which it shares a certain sensibility), the theory
could be interpreted entirely within an anthropocentric and shallow
ethical frame: we should stop destabilizing Gaia simply because that
is dangerous to us. Of course, to the extent that we succeeded in
stopping or sufficiently slowing that process, many species would
thereby also be saved. But it is quite possible to imagine a world that
is stable for most humans, in Gaian terms, but is highly impoverished
in terms of 'biodiversity' – dominated by a few hardy 'weedy
species'.[18] It is also true that Gaia Theory *could* be interpreted ecocentrically with respect to other life-forms and specific, unique
places; but the fact that that would seem to be optional is a weakness.

Gaian holism also presents, it seems to me, a danger of collectivist political authoritarianism. For example, the leap to the Gaian
level is sometimes taken without much evident ethical concern for
the mere organisms, including human, 'down here'. That level, as
far as most personal experience is concerned, is highly abstract; like
'God', 'the nation', 'the people', etc., it therefore leaves an uncomfortable amount of leeway for it to be appropriated for very
different political purposes, and taken in some highly questionable
directions. And the fact that such abstraction is 'scientific' (at least
as far as its principal advocates are concerned), far from undercut-
ting the point just made, simply adds another dimension to its
potential rhetorical power.

Finally, there is Gaia Theory's monism. Lovelock has rightly
condemned 'the three C's' – cars, cows and chainsaws – on account
of their direct contribution to potentially ruinous climate change;

but he cavalierly countenances nuclear energy as no threat, indeed, as a solution. Fastening single-mindedly on Gaian criteria, however, overlooks the ethical significance of other considerations: the potential for nuclear accidents or terrorist strikes resulting in massive long-term environmental pollution and ecological damage (by the standards of organic life) together with lingering deaths and disease (both human and otherwise); the corrosive political effects of the dangerous hypertechnology, enormous expense, unaccountability and secrecy that nuclear power always entails; and so on. These are not ethically neglible considerations, but they find no firm foothold here.

Oddly, Lovelock also overlooks the probability that in addition to these problems, a resurgent nuclear industry would almost certainly continue to be used as an excuse to avoid the energy conservation and efficiency measures, on the demand side, and cheaper, more efficient renewable technologies (wind, wave and solar power), on the supply side, that really do offer a non-life-threatening solution.

I have already praised holism elsewhere and described the individualism of intermediate ecological ethics (for example, animal liberation/rights) as a limitation. Is it therefore inconsistent to criticize Gaia Theory for ignoring the importance of individuals? No. Ecological holism *is* needed; but it is only safe, so to speak, in the hands of those who understand that when it is necessary to wrong certain individuals (that is, overrule their self-perceived interests) in order to defend the common good (upon which *all* depend), it *is* necessary, but that does not make it ethically unproblematic.[19]

In short, ethically speaking, Gaia Theory certainly has powerfully positive ecocentric potential, not least for an ethic of 'global medicine' (although it will take more than a science of 'planetary biology' to realize that goal).[20] Its current limitations, however, seem to indicate that it will need supplementing.

# Deep Ecology

Deep Ecology is both a metaphysical philosophy and a social/cultural movement with political implications. It began as essentially an attempt to work out the principles of ecological activism, rather than as a strictly academic theory. Within the world of contemporary ecological discourse generally, it remains one of the most influential approaches, particularly in America. It was inspired by the work of the Norwegian philosopher Arne Naess, beginning with his paper of 1973, 'The Shallow and the Deep, Long-Range Ecology Movements'. Bill Devall and George Sessions (1985) have also contributed importantly to its development.[21]

The formal basis of Deep Ecology are the *eight Platform Principles* formulated by Naess and Sessions:

1  The flourishing of human and non-human life on Earth has intrinsic value. The value of non-human life-forms is independent of the usefulness these may have for narrow human purposes.
2  Richness and diversity of life-forms are values in themselves and contribute to the flourishing of human and non-human life on Earth.
3  Humans have no right to reduce this richness and diversity except to satisfy vital human needs.
4  Present human interference with the non-human world is excessive, and the situation is rapidly worsening.
5  The flourishing of human life and cultures is compatible with a substantial decrease of the human population. The flourishing of non-human life requires such a decrease.
6  Significant change of life conditions for the better requires change in policies. These affect basic economic, technological and ideological structures.
7  The ideological change is mainly that of appreciating life quality (dwelling in situations of intrinsic value) rather than adhering to a high standard of living. There will be a profound awareness of the difference between big and great.
8  Those who subscribe to the foregoing points have an obligation directly or indirectly to participate in the attempt to implement the necessary changes.[22]

Some of this ground we have discussed in other but related contexts: the distinction between Shallow Ecology or 'environmentalism' and

Deep Ecology (which, indeed, derives from Naess); ecological holism; and the idea of intrinsic value. Subject to what has already been discussed, these important aspects of Deep Ecology need no further comment. One thing which does need to be mentioned, however, is the peculiarity that the Platform Principles make no explicit reference to the Earth as such, emphasizing instead life-forms. That means Deep Ecology could well be identified as a bio-centric mid-green or intermediate ethic. However, I am going to argue that the import of Deep Ecology is ecocentric nonetheless, both in the intentions of its founders and (no less important) how it has been commonly understood. Within the Deep Ecology movement, the terms 'biocentric' and 'ecocentric' tend to be used interchangeably, and it is significant that the main activist movement Deep Ecology has inspired is called 'Earth First!' The common adoption by Deep Ecologists of Leopold's injunction to 'think like a mountain' points to the same conclusion.

Another complication is more serious. Together with Sessions, Naess has outlined a particular instance of a Deep Ecological theory, Ecosophy T, which emphasizes two further principles.[23] In theory, these do not replace the original eight, and remain optional for supporters of Deep Ecology. (As we shall see, the Left Bio group, for example, accept the eight but tend to reject Ecosophy T.) However, Naess himself and others have laid considerable stress on them, and as Kohak perceptively notes, that stress has been accompanied by a perceptible drift in Naess's work since 1973 from a 'Deep Ecology' to a 'Depth Ecology' – as in, depth psychology – that has contributed to the importance of these two principles for the Deep Ecology movement (Kohak 2004: 117).[24] Yet they are also, as we shall see, its most problematic elements. The two principles concerned are as follows.

*Self-realization* (with an upper-case S). The idea here is that the nature of entities is *constituted* by the relations between them, rather than entities being preformed and then establishing relations, or such relations being simply one-way: in Naess's words, a 'relational, total-field image' rather than a 'man-in-the-environment' image. So far so good, but this total field is then conceptualized as one's real Self, as distinct from one's illusory ego-self, and a normative imperative derived: to realize one's Self, i.e., to perceive that that is one's true nature, and to identify with it. (This is a psycho–spiritual process that can be ongoing and take place by degrees.) The hope is that since one's own nature is identical with nature's nature, so to speak, then one would no more harm the natural world unnecessarily than one would harm oneself; and ethics, at least as any kind of rules, becomes redundant.

*Biocentric egalitarianism.* Naess paraphrases this idea as 'the equal right' of life-forms 'to live and blossom'. (It turns out this means ecospherical, or simply ecocentric, egalitarianism.) This seems to be a particular development of ecocentrism which emphasizes not only the value of nature, both human and non–human, but the equality of entities – analogous to human equality despite social class – as instances of such value.

Now some of the criticisms levelled against Deep Ecology do not pass muster. This applies particularly to the vitriolic attacks of Murray Bookchin.[25] For example, Deep Ecology is certainly not necessarily misanthropic (let alone fascist); it simply denies that humans alone have intrinsic value. A more ambiguous question is whether it is inherently quietist, that is, passively anti–political. Given the emphasis on states of consciousness (to which we shall return), that is a dominant theme; however, as the Platform Principles make clear, political action is, at least in principle, also encouraged. Furthermore, Deep Ecology has been a major inspiration to some of the most engaged and effective direct activism in defence of nature in American history.

Some social ecologists and ecofeminists have also charged Deep Ecologists with failing to recognize that contributions of people to ecological destruction are not the same, but wildly unequal (e.g., that of the oil corporation president versus that of the impoverished Third World child), and likewise those who suffer its consequences. This point is certainly valid and should not be lost sight of. But it is also true that there is a common hierarchy of value, which is the essence of anthropocentrism, in which any human being, *simply as such*, has more value than any non–human being. This is the sense in which 'human chauvinism' or 'speciesism' are just as much an ugly reality as racism or sexism.

There has also been intellectual criticism such as that of John Benson, who maintains that the identification with Self demanded by Deep Ecology has three possible senses, all of them unsatisfactory (2000: 126). One is empathy, but this is apparently limited to other intelligent and/or sentient animals, since it 'cannot carry over to plants and mountains'. Here Benson simply assumes, without feeling the need for argument, an individualistic sentience-chauvinism. Second, 'the [natural] object is thought of as partly constitutive of who one is', giving rise to the same kind of concern one feels for oneself. However, 'It is of the essence of such relationships that they are to particular places and beings', and such empathy will therefore not 'take us as far in concern for natural beings as Naess wishes to go'. Here Benson has touched on something important, for it may be that (as I shall argue later) that is as far as anyone *can* go, or *needs* to go, in any kind of ecological context; in which case, Deep Ecologists' calls for a cosmic or cosmological consciousness are mistaken. Third, he points to close human relationships, such that the other person's good is felt to be one's own good. Once again, however – and characteristically of writers even on environmental ethics – Benson dares not venture very far from the modernist anthropocentric redoubt: such empathy, it seems, cannot extend to 'mountains and rivers'. Why not? The work of David Abram (1996) and Anthony Weston (1994) is evidence to the contrary. (Or rather, one kind of evidence, namely convincing arguments; the other kind, equally necessary and more vivid, is personal experience of the natural world beyond the confines of any book, no matter how good.)

Nonetheless, the problems with Ecosophy T that remain are severe. I shall take the two 'basic principles' above in reverse order.

### Biocentric egalitarianism

Ecocentrism is both possible and needed, or so I have argued; but this particular version of it is neither.[26] It is both intellectually and metaphysically implausible – why should value in nature be distributed equally or evenly? (Ironically, there is almost a mechanistic quality to the assumption that it is.)

It is also hopelessly impracticable as a guide to action: you cannot ask anyone (let alone everyone) to live as if literally every life-form – a lethal virus, say – has equal value to all others, including her- or himself; and it offers no guidance, indeed it allows no way, to resolve inevitable conflicts.

Perhaps this is why Naess, under pressure, retreated to the assertion that it was intended 'simply as a statement of non-anthropocentrism', and added the words 'in principle' to its formulation (1989: 28).[27] But in thus trying to correct what was badly formulated from the start, this simply relieves the point of any force at all. What is needed is a coherent and defensible ecocentrism.

### Self-realization

This proposal fares no better.[28] Metaphysical enlightenment and spiritual purity as a supreme value may offer individual salvation, but only at the price of abandoning the rest of the natural world – not exactly the Bodhisattva ideal![29] (Naess has frequently stated that he has been influenced by Buddhism.) The attempt to use 'deep' metaphysics to evade both value and ethics as such can thus only succeed by failing 'ecology'. In short, in trying (however understandably) to counter the tendency for political movements to become dogmatic, programmatic and obsessed with achieving concrete ends while being less than fussy about the means, Ecosophy T has gone too far in the opposite direction. The emphasis on Self-realization as the 'real work' courts New Age idealism and dangerously neglects 'external' consequences and effects; nature, after all, is just as much 'outer' as it is 'inner'.[30]

In ethical terms, that point is, once again, a consequentialist one. But Deep Ecology is just as hostile to deontological ethics, where duties and rules are central. The argument is that people will 'naturally' do the right thing(s) when their apprehension of the natural world is correct, as a result of ever-wider identification of oneself with that world and its fellow inhabitants. This is to ask too much of metaphysics or spirituality. There is no one 'solution' to a problem as complex and deep as ecocide – no royal road, and no promised land; nothing follows automatically from anything else, and at no point are there any guarantees, as some Deep Ecologists seem to imply. When Naess asserts that 'Ethics follow from how we experience the world', and David Rothenberg asks, 'But just how should we experience the world?', that question is as ethical (and specifically deontological) as it is unavoidable.

Significantly, Naess also maintains that 'If Deep Ecology is deep it must relate to our fundamental beliefs, not just to ethics' (1989: 20). But why on Earth cannot ethics be fundamental? Indeed, ultimately, how can it *avoid* being so? Some Deep Ecologists also seem to confuse mora*lity* with mora*lism*. They fail to see that deep ecological insights *and* rules alike can only succeed to the extent that they become an integral part of the political, social and cultural processes of active – and in this case, green – citizenship.[31]

Another problem is that 'Self-realization' is intellectually incoherent. By the nature of discourse, the meaning of any term necessarily depends on what it excludes, what it defines itself against; so to the extent Self is, or becomes, everything, it becomes meaningless. Pure identity via a Big Self is solipcism (absolute egoism and subjective idealism). It also contradicts Naess's own stress elsewhere on relations and pluralism. In practice, too, otherness – recognizing, respecting and valuing differences – is at least as valid and integral to our relationship with nature, as commonality.[32] As we saw in the earlier discussion of ecocentrism, human beings have certain distinctive characteristics vis-à-vis non-human nature, even though these confer no special privileges or superiority (or should not), and are ultimately themselves the work of nature too. To ignore these differences in favour of commonality is dangerous, because it invites a misanthropic ecocentrism which either (1) demands the sacrifice of human distinctiveness as the price of entry to an abstract and collectivized nature, or (2) tries to exclude a demonized humanity from nature. And either way, that programme would amount to an ethical disaster (if it 'succeeded'), or a political disaster (if it failed), opening the door to a reactionary reassertion of anthropocentrism.

'Self-realization' also falsifies an important part of our lives as natural beings who experience themselves as distinct from other natural beings, and the latter as distinct from them. To quote Neil Evernden, 'Wildness is not "ours" – indeed it is the one thing that can never be ours. It is self-willed, independent, and indifferent to our dictates and judgements' (1992: 120). Bill McKibben (1990) has suggested that nature is coming to an end with the effects of human meddling, if not exactly control, becoming unavoidable every-where on the planet. His definition of nature may be questioned, but the undeniable poignancy involved draws its force from deep regret at the passing of what is *not* 'us'.

This is also perceptible in other, more mundane, ways. Was it delightful watching two foxes play, as I did recently, because they were somehow my Self? No. It was delightful because they had nothing to do with me, in any meaningful sense of the word. They were quite unconcerned with me, my will or my desires; they were, in fact, much more important to each other than I was.

Actually, 'Self-realization' is covertly anthropocentric, thus contradicting Deep Ecology's own ecocentrism. It entails a kind of chauvinism in favour of those beings evidently capable of Self-realization, of which humans are by far the most obvious candi-dates. As such, it opens the door, as Val Plumwood has said, to 'an enlargement and extension of egoism' (1995: 160). The New Age version of spiritual Self-realization, selling ancient wisdom to the middle classes, has proven to be highly compatible with the commodification and market capitalism that from one of the chief motors driving ecocide. [33]

As Plumwood also points out, Deep Ecologists have suggested 'that once one has realised that one is indistinguishable from the rainforest, its needs would become one's own. But there is nothing to guarantee this – one could equally well take one's own needs for its' (1995: 160). And indeed, where there is a strong cultural tradition of conflating the social and natural worlds, as with Confucianism, that seems to be exactly what happens: human self-improvement *cannot* conflict with what is regarded as the good of nature.[34] (I would add that, as a matter of fact, people *do* harm themselves, to varying extents, not infrequently. So even if the metaphysics worked, so to speak, it would not necessarily deliver the desired result.)

In short, Sylvan was right: 'The very pedigree of the directive' – to maximize Self-realization – 'should have alerted suspicion. It emerges direct from the humanistic Enlightenment; it is linked to the modern celebration of the individual human, freed from service to higher demands, and also typically from ecological constraints' (Sylvan and Bennett 1994: 154).

An ambitious version of Deep Ecology has been developed by Warwick Fox (1995) under the name of *transpersonal ecology*, with the intention of improving the original while meeting, or under-cutting, the criticisms of feminism and socialism. Unfortunately, his emphasis on replacing a sense of personal self with an 'ontologi-cally' or 'cosmologically' based Self also suffers from the defects just noted. Here too, ecofeminists have been astute critics. Ariel Salleh (1993) notes that Fox's attitude is totalizing in a way that resonates with the anthropocentrism it is supposed to be correcting – and with the *androcentrism* (male-centredness), including its own, that it fails to address.[35] Plumwood (1995, 1993) points out that such a degree of bloodless abstraction ('Being', 'the cosmos', etc.) is an integral part of the anthropocentric, rationalist and masculinist ideology of power over nature. By the same token, it is hostile to just the kind of intimate daily relationship with sensuous natural particulars, and the value of them, that is so important to recover.[36] It is passionate attachments to *particular* places, things and non-humans that move people, and motivate people to defend them. As Plumwood also says, 'It is a short step from the accounts of the ecological [S]elf as the overcoming of "selfish" attachment and particularity . . . to demanding detachment from epistemological location' (2002: 255, n. 19). That step in turn opens the door to the poisoned chalice of techno-scientific 'solutions' to ecological prob-lems; and at least one influential Deep Ecologist, George Sessions (1995), has apparently taken it, sanctioning genetic bioengineering.

Fox argues that 'We can make no firm ontological divide in the field of existence . . . there is no bifurcation in reality between the human and the non-human realms . . . to the extent that we per-ceive boundaries, we fall short of deep ecological consciousness' (1984: 196). But this is to overstate, and thus dangerously distort, the case. The point is not there are *no* boundaries, limits or distinc-tions (we experience these all the time, and they are a part of life it is futile to try to deny). It is rather that they are only *relatively*, not absolutely, real. This is actually another Buddhist point: not the absolute denial of ego, any more than the assertion of its absolute reality, but the Middle Way: the relative, contingent, impermanent nature of Self. (To say that there is a cosmic spirituality superior to mere things is actually to assert that there is an 'emptiness' different or apart from 'form', which is about as close to theological heresy, so to speak, as Buddhism comes.)

Like Naess, Fox also presents transpersonal ecology as a way of bypassing the axiological issue of value-in-nature. He quotes John Seed approvingly: '*It is only by identification with the whole process that correct values will emerge.* Otherwise we see it as self-sacrifice or effort' (Fox 1986: 63; emphasis in original). I'm not sure why self-sacrifice, let alone effort, should be so problematic (as distinct from merely unfashionable); they surely have a part to play. Rules and duties do have their limitations. But such Deep/Transpersonal Ecologists are vulnerable to Gandhi's pointed remark about trying to devise 'a system so perfect that no one will have to be good.'[37] I'm afraid people will always have to try to be good, or at least not to do bad, as well as be actively encouraged to do good, and discouraged from doing bad.

In conclusion, there are very serious problems with Ecosophy T, that is, Naess and Sessions's own version of a Deep Ecological theory. But the ethical heart of Deep Ecology itself, so to speak, is in the right place, and in a world so saturated with anthropocentrism, justifying the domination and exploitation of nature, it continues to offer a lifeline to those seeking an ecocentric alternative. This could perhaps be strengthened by a renewed emphasis on the Platform Principles.

These were condensed and reformulated by the late Stan Rowe in a way which avoids some of the drawbacks just described, and is well worth mentioning:

1  The well-being and flourishing of the living Earth and its many organic/inorganic parts have value in themselves. . . . These values are independent of the usefulness of the non-human world for human purposes.
2  Richness and diversity of Earth's ecosystems, as well as the organic forms that they nurture and support, contribute to the realization of these values and are also values in themselves.
3  Humans have no right to reduce the diversity of Earth's ecosystems and their vital constituents, organic and inorganic.
4  The flourishing of human life and culture is compatible with a substantial decrease of human population. The creative

flourishing of Earth and its multitudinous parts, organic and inorganic, requires such a decrease. (1997: 151)

However, this version, excellent in what it does say, neglects to mention the critical importance of structural social and political change, as well as reducing consumption, and of becoming actively involved in bringing about such changes.

# Deep Green Theory

Richard Sylvan (*né* Routley) has developed a version of Deep Ecology called 'deep green theory' (DGT), which is perhaps one of the most promising yet.[38] DGT shares the key value-orientation of Deep Ecology: '"thinking like a mountain" instead of thinking like a cash register' (Sylvan and Bennett 1994: 182). It is a fully ecocentric ethic, as defined earlier, in which (as already mentioned) the ecological community is identical with the ethical community (ibid. 91). Its holism is benign, not that of a forced collectivity, and its emphasis is on the common good of communities, including that of individuals – up to the point where their activities threaten the former, upon which all depend. DGT also shares the more specific import of the four reformulated points of Deep Ecology just quoted. Unlike Naess and Session's version of Deep Ecology, however, it is a fully and overtly *ethical* theory, with these characteristics:

- All established or traditional ethics are recognized as inadequate, ecologically speaking.
- The human chauvinism of both the Sole Value Assumption and the Greater Value Assumption is rejected, so the intrinsic value of natural items can, in particular situations, override strictly human interests.
- The human/non-human distinction is *not ethically significant*; in fact, no single species, class or characteristic (whether sentience, life or whatever) serves to justify special ethical treatment, or to deny it. This eco-impartiality, however, does not entail trying to adhere to equal value or treatment in specific situations.

Nor does it try to rule out human use of the environment – 'only too much use and use of too much' (ibid. 147). It follows, to pick just one example, that sustainable indigenous inhabitation and use of remaining wildernesses is perfectly acceptable, and indeed potentially a key to their preservation; but indigenous industrial development and/or commercial exploitation, unrestrained by ecological considerations, is *not*.[39] Similarly, broadly sustainable hunting for the pot is one thing; the 'bushmeat' trade in Africa that is now threatening whole species, for profit, is something very different. (The ecological effects of development/exploitation are not affected by who its agents are, and, to that important extent, charges of elitism or ethnocentrism are therefore beside the point.[40] But an ecocentric perspective, such as that of DGT, is required in order to recognize this fact.)

- 'What is required now is that reasons be given *for* interfering with the environment, rather than reasons for not doing so' (Sylvan and Bennett 1994: 147) – a point that becomes more urgently true with every passing year. Or, as Midgley puts it, from an ecocentric point of view, 'the burden of proof is not on someone who wants to preserve mahogany trees from extinction. It is on the person who proposes to destroy them' (1997: 96).

- 'The implementation of environmental ethics is a top-down and bottom-up and inside out issue. . . . Achieving individual change . . . is a start, but it is not enough. Institutional change is also required. It is not enough that individuals may want to change practices in their own lives. The community in which they live must meet their needs by offering environmentally sound alternatives' (Sylvan and Bennett 1994: 180).

These points have specific and important economic and fiscal implications, such as replacing profit maximization with profit satisization (i.e., sufficiency) and so-called free markets with fair. Sylvan and Bennett's political analysis, including an ecocentric programme for change, is wide-ranging and astute. Here the contrast with Naess and Session's Ecosophy T is striking; nonetheless, Sylvan, accepting the eight-point Platform, viewed DGT as part of the Deep Ecology movement.

There is considerable detail in Sylvan and Bennett's work about the political, cultural and educational ways in which DGT could – and to become influential, must – be realized as ethical virtue in the practices of green citizenship. They recognize, rightly, that you should not have to be a saint to be ecologically virtuous, but that an ecological society in which such virtue is normal will only come about through a great deal of hard individual and collective work. It will not result from metaphysical enlightenment alone, although a spiritual practice can certainly be part of such work. But this is not the place to go into detail, so I urge readers to seek out their book.

They also point out that, as I have already implied, there are circumstances in which arguments of a shallow and intermediate type may well be appropriate to invoke; deep green ethics is not meant to cancel these out or replace them, but to reach the places they cannot. The same applies to individual and rights-based approaches. Conversely, however, the absence of deep green ethics makes the current vogue for largely cosmetic measures like 'environmental modernization' – what Rudolph Bahro aptly called 'cleaning the teeth of the dragon' – all too easy.[41]

There is one major point about which I think Sylvan was mistaken, and that is his rejection of reverence for nature in favour of mere 'respect'. For the reasons mentioned earlier in connection with Plumwood's criticism of transpersonal ecology, ecocentrism cannot afford to sacrifice emotional, spiritual and cultural valuing of specific wild places, or, even more importantly, the wild *in* places. As a philosopher (and, perhaps, as a male philosopher), Sylvan's own attachment to rationalism is understandable; but here, ironically, it weakens his own case. We shall return to this point later.

It is puzzling why, given that Sylvan's work is of high quality, original and uncompromising, he is so neglected in ethical-ecological discourse. Perhaps the problem is that last point. In any case, the little criticism he has received so far (such as that of Grey 2000) has been thin and unconvincing. The 'weaknesses' Grey identifies will arguably be true of *any* normative ethical discourse, and, ironically, Grey's own narrowly academic rationalism rules out one serious criticism that could be made of Sylvan: that his own severely intellectual style of writing was sometimes at odds with the import of his message.

## Left Biocentrism

This is a green philosophy and activist movement (both are equally emphasized) which initially grew out of the work of an activist and writer in Canada, David Orton.[42] His website 'The Green Web'[43] led to an internet discussion group, now the 'Left Bio' list, whose members agreed a primer of points in collective discussions culminating in March 1998. Now, general agreement is the basis for membership, and there is considerable and lively discussion of the problems facing those trying to build an ecocentric movement. (The 'bio' of the name is ambiguous, often being used to mean 'eco'.)[44]

This collective character is one of the distinctive aspects of Left Biocentrism, both internally, as a group, and as a movement that explicitly identifies itself as working within the larger Deep Ecology movement, accepts both its ecocentric values and the eight-point Platform, and speaks respectfully of Naess. At the same time, the Left Bio emphasis is quite distinct. Its other main inspiration (the 'Left' part) is that of social justice, political radicalism (both socialist and anarchist) and revolutionary idealism, and its other influences include Richard Sylvan, Rudolf Bahro and Andrew McLaughlin.

Rather than believing an ecological society can come entirely from individual change, psycho-spiritual or otherwise, Left Bios recognize that our problems – and therefore any real solution to them – are structural or systemic. Without diminishing the necessity of personal responsibility and initiative, they see that our current collective addiction to overconsumption, overpopulation and technical fixes is a context of irresponsibility that undercuts individual efforts.[45] A truly sustainable society requires social and political structures that actively encourage ecologically virtuous practices by enough individuals, and discourage the contrary, to make a real difference.

As to whether such a society could be achieved 'within' a capitalist framework, there are obviously large questions attached to what is defined as capitalist; but even so, this must surely remain a very difficult question.[46] In any case, from a Left Bio perspective, capitalism and socialism are two sides of the same coin: two different aspects of, and responses to, the same process, whose proper name is ***industrialism***.[47] The socialist end of the spectrum is the more humane and intelligent (potentially, at least!), and to that extent is therefore preferable, but both are anthropocentric, and thus share the same blind spot regarding ecocentrism. Adherents of Left Bio retain that preference but no longer believe that all 'our' problems are resolvable within an anthropocentric ambit – or that human problems are the only ones that matter.

A Left Bio perspective is also aware that saving biotic systems will result in harm to humans that is unequally distributed, those with the least resources suffering most. It therefore urges that the latter be actively considered in any transition to an ecologically steady-state society. That point, however, must not be used as an excuse to duck the whole issue.[48]

By the same token – and this is another significant departure from its other main source, the traditions of social democracy, socialism and anarchism – Left Biocentrism is keenly aware of the ecological limits of anthropocentric social justice. It is certainly not that social justice is unimportant or irrelevant, just that they 'are not the *whole* answer, and probably not the primary reason we humans are so far out of balance with what might be sustainable'.[49] (After all, some human societies destroyed their and others' environments long before capitalism.) Concerns with class, gender and race, while urgent, are therefore viewed in the context of *ecological* justice. The goal, as Orton puts it, is 'solidarity with all life, not just human life'. In this view, nature, not labour power, is the principal source of wealth, and that wealth is shared with other life-forms. It is a true commons – even, as such, sacred – and therefore fundamentally 'not to be privatised'.[50]

As that last point implies, most Left Bios also reject the secularism and/or atheism of traditional leftism. But they also tend to be critical of both traditional religion, on the one hand, and fully privatized spirituality on the other. Instead, Left Biocentrism affirms a 'collective spirituality' based on the ultimate value of the Earth and its life-forms. The connection with politics is the power of such a perception, both individually and shared, to inspire and sustain a defence of the Earth and its life. It is fair to say, however, that this subject remains one of occasional heated exchanges on the list. (We shall return to it in chapter 9.)

## The Left Biocentrism primer

Here is the text which Left Bios have agreed:

1  Left biocentrism is a left focus or theoretical tendency within the Deep Ecology movement, which is subversive of the existing industrial society. It accepts and promotes the eight-point Deep Ecology Platform drawn up by Arne Naess and George Sessions. Left biocentrism holds up as an ideal, identification, solidarity, and compassion with all life. 'Left' as used in left biocentrism, means anti-industrial and anti-capitalist, but not necessarily socialist. The expressions 'left biocentrism' or 'left ecocentrism' are used interchangeably.

2  Left biocentrism accepts the view that the Earth belongs to no one. While raising a number of criticisms, left biocentrism is meant to strengthen, not undermine, the Deep Ecology movement which identifies with all life.

3  Left biocentrism says that individuals must take responsibility for their actions and be socially accountable. Part of being individually responsible is to practise voluntary simplicity, so as to minimize one's own impact upon the Earth.

4  Left biocentrists are concerned with social justice and class issues, but within a context of ecology. To move to a Deep Ecology world, the human species must be mobilized, and a concern for social justice is a necessary part of this mobilization. Left biocentrism is for the redistribution of wealth, nationally and internationally.

5  Left biocentrism opposes economic growth and consumerism. Human societies must live within ecological limits so that all other species may continue to flourish. We believe that

bioregionalism, not globalism, is necessary for sustainability. The perspective of the late German Green philosopher Rudolf Bahro is accepted that, for worldwide sustainability, industrialized countries need to reduce their impact upon the Earth to about one tenth of what it is at the present time. It is also incumbent upon non-industrialized nations to become sustainable and it is necessary for industrialized nations to help on this path.

6 Left biocentrism holds that individual and collective spiritual transformation is important to bring about major social change, and to break with industrial society. We need inward transformation, so that the interests of all species override the short-term self-interest of the individual, the family, the community, and the nation.

7 Left biocentrism believes that Deep Ecology must be applied to actual environmental issues and struggles, no matter how socially sensitive, e.g., population reduction, aboriginal issues, workers' struggles, etc.

8 Social ecology, ecofeminism and eco-Marxism, while raising important questions, are all human-centred and consider human-to-human relations within society to be more important and, in the final analysis, determine society's relationship to the natural world. Left biocentrism believes that an egalitarian, non-sexist, non-discriminating society, a highly desirable goal, can still be exploitive towards the Earth.

9 Left biocentrists are 'movement greens' in basic orientation. They are critical of existing Green political parties, which have come to an accommodation with industrial society and have no accountability to the Deep Ecology movement.

10 To be politically relevant, Deep Ecology needs to incorporate the perspective advanced by left biocentrism.

It is too soon to discern the exact impact of Left Biocentrism, but I am tempted to say, the more the better. In any case, its explicitly ethical and political focus corrects the most serious single blind spot of other and hitherto better-known versions of the Deep Ecology movement. The Left Bio movement is also well placed, by virtue of its dual ancestry, to put ecology onto the progressive political agenda, where it is now glaringly absent. Extraordinary as it may seem, feminists, anti-racists and socialists are almost as likely as those on the neo-liberal and anti-democratic right to ignore the claims of even mid-range ecological ethics (e.g., animals), let alone ecocentric ethics. This fact is sadly evident in the programmes of nearly all today's so-called green parties, where the green values are strictly shallow, that is, advocated insofar as they further human interests, and not when they exceed them, let alone conflict. (Please recall, in this connection, Bahro's words when resigning from the German Greens.)

Further evidence, if needed, comes from the present apparently enlightened and progressive government of Brazil, under 'Lula' da Silva, which is currently advancing with the destruction of the Amazonian rainforest – 2003 was one of the worst years ever – and its forced conversion to cattle ranching for meat and agricultural production: mainly soya, including GM, for foreign markets. This should not be surprising, considering the anthropocentric and modernist (both statist and technological) lineage of Marxism.[51] This is not to say the latter's concerns and critical points are not often valid, nor that sexism and racism do not need combating either. But consider the following points.

First, at present, humans – roughly 0.5 per cent of the total biomass of the Earth – are consuming, directly or indirectly, at least 20 per cent of the total net product of its terrestrial photosynthetic energy (along with about 50 per cent of the accessible runoff of fresh water).[52] This is truly anthropocentrism in action: a single species has already appropriated for its sole use at least a quarter of the planet's energy, upon which *all* life depends. In other words, humanity is behaving like the biological equivalent – and *ethical*, assuming humans have any choice (which most of us, including those on the left, would like to think) – of a capitalist upper class, master race or patriarchy. Is there really nothing for a progressive agenda to address here?

Second, it is possible to imagine a world devoid of most species which do not directly or indirectly serve human interests, and of any places which qualify as wild, but in which (although this is harder to imagine) any significant degrees of racism, sexism and inequality do not exist; a world, in other words, in which the pro-gressive anthropocentric agenda has largely been realized but is nonetheless ecologically severely impoverished at best, and a disaster at worst.

In fact, that outcome would (will?) take any politically progressive agenda down with it – not only ultimately, because of our dependence as organisms on ecological dynamics, but well before then, because of the social and political effects of ecocrisis: from the social stress and disorder, to outright war, resulting from competition, within as well as between countries, for increasingly scarce resources.

Third, when there are direct conflicts between jobs and the economy on the one hand and threatened non-human nature (e.g., old-growth forest) on the other, we know from historical experience how rarely the latter wins, and how tenuous those few victories are: 'the long defeat', indeed.[53] And the interests of unionized or collectivized labour, in *this* war, put it on the same side as the rest of the anthropocentric forces.[54]

Finally, the simple and still, it seems, unpalatable, fact is that (as Sandy Irvine (2001) once put it), from the Earth's point of view, the effects of an armoured personnel carrier and an ambulance are indistinguishable. However preferable the latter may be (and it is), both remain with an ambit – anthropocentrism – that urgently needs an additional, wider and deeper perspective. Defending the public sphere, however important, is not enough; the common good can no longer be restricted to humanity alone (Curry 2000).

## The Earth Manifesto

Two Canadian ecologists/naturalists loosely associated with the Left Bio network have recently produced another deep green manifesto with an even more explicitly ecocentric emphasis. They are Ted Mosquin[55] and the late Stan Rowe.[56] *A Manifesto For Earth* was published in 2004. It sets out a worldview, with its corresponding ethic and broadly sketched programme, that shifts the focus 'from humanity to the Ecosphere', identified as that 'life-giving matrix' (including its nonorganic components) that is the source of *all* its organisms, sustains them, and to which they ultimately return.

They characterize the dominant contrary view as homocentric (i.e., anthropocentric), and point out that 'Humanity's 10,000-year-old experiment in mode-of-living at the expense of Nature, culminating in economic globalization, is failing. A primary reason is that we have placed the importance of our species above all else.' But like the other dark green ethics discussed here, this one is critical of human chauvinism, not humans as such.

There is a vital place for wonder here, and a sense of the sacred, but not for the off-planet spirituality that characterizes most theistic (and New Age) religions. Similarly, this Earth is not an abstract concept to be wilfully manipulated and 'managed', but a profoundly complex and intricate affair, whose local and regional particularities are of the essence. One can only work *with* them. 'The goal is restoration of Earth's diversity and beauty, with our prodigal species once again a cooperative, responsible, ethical member.' (The resonances with Gaia Theory, Land Ethic and Deep Ecology need no emphasis.)

The principles of the Earth Manifesto cannot be quoted in full here, but this is a basic outline, with excerpts and a few comments. It is so new as to render further critical discussion at this point premature.

## Core principles

1  *The Ecosphere is the Centre of Value for Humanity.* 'Comprehension of the ecological reality that people are Earthlings, shifts the center of values away from the homocentric to the ecocentric, from *Homo sapiens* to Planet Earth.' As the authors rightly point out, 'Without attention to the priority of Earth-as-context, biocentrism easily reverts to a chauvinistic homocentrism, for who among all animals is commonly assumed to be the wisest and best?'

2  *The Creativity and Productivity of Earth's Ecosystems Depend on their Integrity.* 'The evolutionary creativity and continued productivity of Earth and its regional ecosystems require the continuance of their key structures and ecological processes.'

3  *The Earth-centred Worldview is supported by Natural History.* (It is

good to see natural history, as distinct from modern biology, restored to prominence.)

4  *Ecocentric Ethics is Grounded in Awareness of our Place in Nature,* which brings with it 'a sense of connectedness and reverence for the abundance and vitality of sustaining Nature'.

5  *An Ecocentric Worldview Values Diversity of Ecosystems and Cultures.* 'An ecocentric worldview values Earth's diversity in all its forms, the non-human as well as the human.' The corresponding ethic 'challenges today's economic globalization that ignores the ecological wisdom embedded in diverse cultures, and for short-term profit destroys them.'

6  *Ecocentric Ethics Supports Social Justice.* Social ecologists rightly attack inequalities that hurt relatively powerless humans but fail to consider 'the current rapid degradation of Earth's ecosystems that increases inter-human tensions while foreclosing possibilities for sustainable living and for the elimination of poverty'.

## Action principles

7  *Defend and Preserve Earth's Creative Potential.* Barring cosmic collisions, 'Earth's evolving inventiveness will continue for millions of years, hampered only where humans have destroyed whole ecosystems by exterminating species or by toxifying sediments, water and air'. Therefore activities that do so – especially lethal technologies and industries, 'enriching special corporate interests, and satisfying human wants rather than needs' – 'need to be identified and publicly condemned'.

8  *Reduce Human Population Size.* 'A primary cause of ecosystem destruction and species extinctions is the burgeoning human population that already far exceeds ecologically sustainable levels.' Every additional human adds to the immense pressure on inherently limited resources (renewable as well as non-renewable), especially in the overdeveloped world where consumption is highest.

9  *Reduce Human Consumption of Earth's Parts.* 'The chief threat

to the Ecosphere's diversity, beauty and stability is the ever-increasing appropriation of the planet's goods for exclusive human uses. Such appropriation and over-use, often justified by population overgrowth, steals the livelihood of other organisms.' Our vital needs do not amount to a 'license to plunder and exterminate'.

10 *Promote Ecocentric Governance.* 'In present centers of power, who speaks for wolf? and who speaks for temperate rain forest? Such questions have more than metaphorical significance; they reveal the necessity of legally safeguarding the many vital non-human components of the Ecosphere.' New bodies of law, policy, and administration are required as 'embodiments of the ecocentric philosophy, ushering in ecocentric methods of governance'.

11 *Spread the Message.* 'Those who agree with the preceding principles have a duty to spread the word by education and leadership. The initial urgent task is to awaken all people to their functional dependence on Earth's ecosystems as well as their bonds to all other species.'

Completely independently, *The Earth Charter* appeared in 2000.[57] It was a statement of sixteen ethical principles 'for building a just, sustainable and peaceful global society in the 21st Century'. These principles are intended to be widely (although not necessarily universally) shared, in order to provide a basis for 'defining sustainable development in terms of global ethics' (Lynn 2004: 2, 3). The Charter has been recognized by UNESCO and will be, at the time of writing, adopted by the IUCN/World Conservation Union.

The Charter begins with an ecocentric recognition of the Earth as our home, and therefore the protection of its vitality, diversity and beauty as 'a sacred trust'. It also points to the deteriorating global situation respecting both natural and human communities. It names the primary challenge of our times as forming a 'global partnership' to bring about '[f]undamental changes . . . in our values, institutions, and ways of living'. Finally, it calls for 'a sense of universal responsibility, identifying ourselves with the whole Earth community as well as our local communities'.

Here are the principles themselves, reduced to just their headings:[58]

I. *Respect and Care for the Community of Life*
   1. Respect Earth and life in all its diversity . . .
   2. Care for the community of life with understanding, compassion, and love . . .
   3. Build democratic societies that are just, participatory, sustainable, and peaceful . . .
   4. Secure Earth's bounty and beauty for present and future generations . . .

II. *Ecological Integrity*
   5. Protect and restore the integrity of Earth's ecological systems, with special concern for biological diversity and the natural processes that sustain life . . .
   6. Prevent harm as the best method of environmental protection and, when knowledge is limited, apply a precautionary approach . . .
   7. Adopt patterns of production, consumption, and reproduction that safeguard Earth's regenerative capacities, human rights, and community well-being . . .
   8. Advance the study of ecological sustainability and promote the open exchange and wide application of the knowledge acquired . . .

III. *Social and Economic Justice*
   9. Eradicate poverty as an ethical, social, and environmental imperative . . .
   10. Ensure that economic activities and institutions at all levels promote human development in an equitable and sustainable manner . . .
   11. Affirm gender equality and equity as prerequisites to sustainable development and ensure universal access to education, health care, and economic opportunity . . .
   12. Uphold the right of all, without discrimination, to a natural and social environment supportive of human dignity, bodily health, and spiritual well-being, with special attention to the rights of indigenous people and minorities . . .

IV. *Democracy, Nonviolence, and Peace*

13. Strengthen democratic institutions at all levels, and provide transparency and accountability in governance, inclusive participation in decision-making, and access to justice . . .

14. Integrate into formal education and life-long learning the knowledge, values, and skills needed for a sustainable way of life . . .

15. Treat all living beings with respect and consideration . . .

16. Promote a culture of tolerance, nonviolence, and peace . . .

Now it can hardly be doubted that these principles specify admirable and desirable ends in a comprehensive way; nor that the recommended means are appropriate. And such documents involve a great deal of painstaking work which should be recognized and applauded. But there is a problem here which grows out of the very comprehensiveness and generality that the goal of 'widespread agreement' requires. It is difficult to believe that what approaches being a progressive wish-list which includes nature *and* social justice *and* peace *and* democracy *and* diversity will have much real impact in and on the world of concrete particulars. (Genuine world-government – and even that assumes a benign and competent world-government – might provide the conditions in which it could acquire such influence, including some teeth, but we remain very far from that.)

This problem has another serious aspect, which is that the Earth Charter fails to admit the possibility of conflict in actual cases – always possible, and virtually inevitable – between these various ideals, especially between the interests of human and non-human nature. It thus falls short of an ecocentric ethic as I have defined it above, and as compared with the Manifesto for Earth. And strategically speaking, the overwhelmingly dominant ethical consensus is anthropocentric and/or light green at best: an imbalance that urgently needs redressing. So Mosquin and Rowe's more uncompromising stance, which firmly places human concerns within an ecocentric context, is preferable. This is not just a strategic point; we do all live on (or rather, in, since it includes the breathable atmosphere), and depend on, the Earth. Despite its virtues, that is a truth which the Charter makes it too easy to ignore or fudge in practice; whereas the Manifesto, quite rightly, makes it that much harder.

# Ecofeminism

Perhaps even more than the other schools of thought and action in this section, ecofeminism is rich and complex in ways – including disagreements, or at least different emphases (not necessarily a weakness) – that are difficult to encompass within the necessary simplifications of an introduction. In addition, placing it in this company is bound to be controversial, for it is not necessarily eco-centric (nor would all ecofeminists necessarily want to be seen as such). Nonetheless, I believe there is a strong case for including it: namely that the *effects* of genuine ecofeminism are ecocentric, and invaluably so.

Rather like Left Biocentrism, ecofeminism is a meeting of two strands. One is feminism itself: the awareness of the pathological effects of dominant **patriarchal** or (to use a more recent term) **masculinist** structures, both 'inner' and 'outer' – particularly, of course, on women but also, ultimately, on their oppressors – and the attempt to replace them with ones that also value the feminine. ('Masculinist' bears the same relationship to 'masculine' as 'rational-ist', for example, does to 'rational'; that is, it takes a natural or normal human attribute and turns it into the supervalued centre-piece of an ideology.) Another way to put it would be that such structures and attitudes are **androcentric** (man-centred). In this central respect, feminism is an anthropocentric concern and ethic; at least, there is nothing necessarily ecocentric about it.

The other influence, however, is a recognition of, and deep concern about, the equally masculinist domination and exploitation of nature, through the same habitual structures of thought, feeling and action that devalue and harm women. Thus ecofeminism brings to the critique of that pathology a dimension which is missing from all the others we have so far encountered: gender. Ecofeminists have performed an invaluable service in bringing to our attention the way gender, often unconsciously, is deeply implicated in the ecological crisis – not only in the macro-level pathologies of ecological devastation but also in the minute practices and assumptions of daily life. The connections with industrial capital, in both ways, are also clear.

There is something of a division of labour in this respect, with some authors (like Plumwood and, allowing for other differences, Karren J. Warren) tending to more philosophical 'idealist' analyses and others (such as Salleh and Maria Mies) working in a more political and economic 'materialist' vein. But in both aspects, the case for combining an ecofeminist perspective with ecocentrism is strong – not as replacing the concern with anthropocentrism, but as partly a refinement of it and partly an additional dynamic.[59]

One way of understanding the key role of gender in generating ecocrisis is through the metaphor of a ***master mentality***. Always present throughout human history, it was given an enormous boost by the advent of modernity – that is, by the same processes, at the same time (beginning in the mid-seventeenth century), that licensed the capitalist and techno-scientific exploitation of nature. So of what does this mentality, including its institutionalized forms, consist?

Basically, it draws on some very old ways of thinking and valuing, which Warren (1993) has analysed as: dualism, whereby all life is ordered into two opposing categories; value-laden hierarchies, whereby such dualism is not neutral, but what is 'up' has more value than what is 'down'; and the role of what is 'lower' is to serve the needs of what is 'higher'.[60]

But what of the specific content? The relevant dualisms, with the 'superior' first, are: humanity versus nature; male versus female; and reason versus emotion. (This becomes indistinguishable from abstract intellect versus the body, rationality versus irrationality, etc.)

These value-laden hierarchies draw heavily on old sources, especially Greek philosophy and Christianity, but it was, as I have just suggested, most effectively formulated by the fathers of the Scientific Revolution, especially Bacon, Descartes and Galileo.[61] And while reason is taken as the 'highest' aspect of being human – thus implicitly but firmly excluding women – scientific rationality presents itself in turn as the ultimate expression of reason. It would indeed be extraordinary, then, if the ideology of modern science was not deeply prejudiced against both women and nature.[62]

This, then, is the upshot:

*humanity* = *male* = *reason*, over and against *nature* = *female* = *emotion*.

In short, the domination and exploitation of nature and women proceed by the same logic, the same processes and, by and large, the same people. As Plumwood (1995) says, 'What is taken to be authentically and characteristically human, defining of the human, as well as the ideal for which humans should strive, is not to be found in what is shared with the natural and animal (e.g., the body, sexuality, reproduction, emotionality, the senses, agency) but in what is thought to separate and distinguish them – especially reason and its offshoots' (quoted in Benson 2000: 122).

Here, let us note three additional points. First, the actual processes of gender are messier and more complicated than the logic, and the people even more so; for example, men certainly dominate, but those dominating also include a few women. But the fact remains that even when women do get to be represented, and indeed do some of the representing, the structural terms of how society is organized and run tend to remain masculinist.

Second, the role of gender, including the structures and sensibilities that entail a masculinist bias, is indeed fundamental to ongoing ecocrisis. It is very difficult to imagine the latter being able to proceed without the kind of attitude, institutionalized and normalized, that Teresa Brennan (2000) calls 'sadodispassionate'. The only qualification is that gender should not be considered the *only* cause, and in any given actual situation, the extent to which it is directly implicated – even if it is almost always present – will vary. (There are no a priori guarantees here, any more than with respect to other dynamics.)

Third, however close the connection between women and nature may be, and therefore their joint suppression, it is best viewed as contingent. To see it as essential or 'necessary' (whether on mystical, biological or other grounds) would be problematic, for two reasons. First, that is the very argument long used by male chauvinists to justify dominating women. And second, to exalt women-as-nature rather than despising them, while preferable, merely *inverts* the dominant values attached to male/female essentialism; it preserves the same destructive logic, when the point is to *sub*vert it wholesale. Any populist version of ecofeminism that inflated the feminine and demonized the masculine, while it might be a refreshing change for some, would not be much of an ethical advance on the reverse. Nor would leaving women still supposedly less 'rational' than men, and men less 'emotional' than women.

More promising, therefore, is the work of finding ways to extend and strengthen generally ways of perceiving, valuing and treating the natural world that have long been characterized as feminine, without subscribing to an essentialist determinism which would deny men the ability to change their ways or share in such a process. As a key part of that, women's experience and insights can be appreciated as special and important without being therefore morally superior. As Salleh writes, 'It is nonsense to assume that women are any closer to nature than men. The point is that women's reproductive labour and such patriarchally assigned work roles as cooking and cleaning bridge men and nature in a very obvious way, and one that is denigrated by patriarchal culture' (1992: 208).

The case for combining an ecofeminist critique of androcentrism with ecocentrism is strong.[63] The former does not replace the concern that Deep Ecologists and other ecocentrics have with anthropocentrism; it refines and arguably deepens that concern. And the effects of ecofeminist experience and insights are potentially deeply ecocentric. They include ways of being and behaving in the world without which, I believe, ecocentrism must fail: an appreciation and reassertion, against modernist abstract universalism, the value of life as embodied and embedded, situated and engaged, local and particular; and against an inflated rationalism, the value of intuition and feelings; and finally, the potential importance and value of what cannot be rationally calculated, economically or otherwise.[64]

Non-exclusive and non-essentialist ecofeminism thus has powerfully positive resonances with the other ecocentric schools/movements analysed here. It also relates closely to the kind of ethics I have described as having the greenest potential: virtue ethics. (Not coincidentally, this is a kind that predates modernity, and promises, by the same token, to survive it best.) Under the term an ***ethics of care***, some feminists have moved away from the abstract universalism of both deontology and utilitarianism, and articulated instead the kind of ethical relationships that connect people, especially but not only women, to the world in situated and contextual ways.[65] This opens the way to recognize that valuing, caring for and protecting the natural world proceed best from particular, sensuous, emotional and (in a related, materialist sense) spiritual involvements with it. The attitude of 'holding', to use Sara Ruddick's term, that maintains a household, nurtures a child and sustains a network of mutually supportive relationships, is equally suited to 'world protection, world-preservation, world repair' (Ruddick 1989: 79, quoting Adrienne Rich).

Furthermore, as Plumwood writes, 'There is no good reason to think that the particularistic kinds of ethical relations feminists have discussed are any less relevant to interspecies ethics than to intra-human ethics, that these interspecies relationships are of necessity any less multidimensional, complex, rich and varied than our relationships with humans, or any more reducible to single parameters like rights' (2002: 187).

There is much profound food for thought here – and for action – with an ecofeminist ethic of care, on the one hand, potentially converging with the character orientation of virtue ethics, notwithstanding its more masculine origins in civic republicanism. But it is important to realize that, as Salleh reminds us, such work is presently being undertaken and performed by women worldwide, although it is relatively undervalued, unrecognized and untheorized. This labour not only makes such women indispensable in a global struggle to realize ecocentric values; it means that a vital basis for an ecocentric virtue ethic, not of laws nor of calculations but of character, *already exists*. And in a world littered with the wrecks and casualties of grand abstract schemes, that may be the most promising as well as most realistic place to start.[66]

# 9

## Deep Green Ethics as Post-Secular

### Dogmatic Secularism

As I mentioned earlier, Deep Green Theory rejects 'reverence' for nature in favour of less demanding 'respect'. Given the serious problems with the established religions, including their very poor ecological record, one can see why, but Sylvan's move seems nonetheless a mistake. The problem is twofold: (1) strategically, secular 'respect' is much weaker and therefore potentially less effective; and (2) substantively, an emotional-spiritual dimension is present everywhere in both ecological and anti-ecological discourse, and trying to deny that only makes it harder to recognize and encourage or criticize it, as necessary.

One thing secularism obscures is that the ideology that justifies most of modernity's onslaught on nature – 'progress', meaning strictly human progress (and in practice, only for some humans) – is, for most of its most influential adherents, a crypto-religion. Listen to the leaders of the G8, World Trade Organization or the World Bank, for example, and it is quite clear that they are fuelled by a faith. Conversely, and equally importantly, when people value nature strongly enough to act to protect it, they do so in a way that is *in effect* religious and, as such, stronger than mere respect. It has to be, in order to resist the all-too-available blandishments of utilitarian appeals to 'rational' self-interest. That is why advocates of the latter call their green opponents 'sentimental', 'nostalgic', 'emotional' and so on: in short, 'irrational'. Note too the way this mindset and strategy are powerfully gendered, with every term of opprobrium an implicitly feminine one, and thus – given the 'problems' posed by embodiment – also anti-Earth.

But secularism has a powerful grip on the modern mindset, including those on the political 'left', even when they are trying to oppose the industrial megamachine. Kate Soper's book *What Is Nature?*, for example, argues a socialist case for protecting nature, but it culminates in a rant against 'irrational forms of superstition': 'We cannot seek to protect nature by pretending to forms of belief that have been exploded by the march of science and technology.' Monsanto and Exxon could ask for no more. Typical of most 'progressive' secular intellectuals, she concludes with the fallacious assumption that reverence for nature is *necessarily* misanthropic (1995: 274–5, 277).

Similarly, Murray Bookchin (1995), the founder of social ecology, has inveighed against such reverence, charging it with everything from superstition, mystification, authoritarianism and fascism to (inevitably) Nazism.[1] Bookchin has long identified market commodity capitalism as the single biggest enemy of both nature and humanity, yet somehow he failed to notice that it acts hand-in-glove with rationalist-realist scientism (which we discussed briefly earlier, in the section on 'Secular Ethics' in chapter 3). His argument thus becomes indistinguishable from the attacks on ecocentrism by neo-liberals – like Anna Bramwell (1989) – and conservative anthropocentrists – like Luc Ferry (1995).

What really reveals how pervasive a secularist ideology is among intellectuals, however, is the fact that even one of Bookchin's most acute critics, Robyn Eckersley, shares the same blind spot. She realizes that 'Conforming to the requirements and modes of rationality of the dominant culture has rarely served the interests of diverse minority cultures' (1998: 171), to say nothing of non-human natures. Yet almost in the same breath, she rejects any spiritual defence of nature, since 'it would seem more appropriate nowadays to find a secular (and scientifically informed), public justification for government action to protect the environment' (ibid. 178) – as if secular scientific discourse had played no part in the rationality of today's dominant culture.

John Benson, in his book on environmental ethics, takes an apparently sensible, balanced position on this question. He supports a *naturalistic* view of nature, which he defines as 'a view that is agnostic about the existence of supernatural beings of any kind and is broadly consistent with current scientific theory'. 'Nature' is then defined as 'the whole material universe', in which case 'The only possible beings outside of nature in this sense are supernatural beings, such as gods, which are defined negatively as non-spatial and non-temporal' (2000: 120). This sounds reasonable enough until you stop to consider what is smuggled into the argument as unargued assumption. Even if it is granted that nature is material or physical in the modern sense – devoid of agency, subjectivity or indeed life as such – why should it be *only* material? No reason is given. Nor can (for example) a scientific answer be given, for either science has nothing to say about what it cannot detect and measure; or it does, but then its pronouncements are no longer scientific ones, because they depend on a wide range of assumptions and values that cannot themselves be supported scientifically without already assuming the truth or value of science.[2] And in that case, why should the only possible spiritual beings be 'supernatural' ones, that is, outside nature and therefore non-spatial and non-temporal?

In fact, the idea of nature as purely material, and implicitly mechanistic, is by no means self-evident or axiomatic. It only gained power, and then common currency, as a result of a long and complex intellectual, social and political power struggle beginning in the mid-seventeenth century. Previously, for the vastly longer part of human history and for many if not most people, nature had a spiritual dimension that was, and to some still is, as obvious as its materiality. This materiality, as Plumwood writes, 'is already full of form, spirit, story, agency, and glory' (2002: 226).

But the fundamental flaw with any discussion such as Benson's (which is the usual kind) is its uncritical acceptance of a firm distinction between 'material' and 'spiritual'. That very assumption, inherited from Platonism, Christianity and modern science almost unchanged, is just the problem. (That religion exalts one side of the opposition and science the other is ultimately irrelevant.) We shall never be able to understand and appreciate nature until we re-learn to see it as *both* 'spiritual' subject and 'natural' object.[3]

## An Ecocentric Spirituality

It is true (as I noted earlier) that the world's major religions all fall short, in their traditional and, for the most part, present forms, of anything resembling an ecological ethic. Furthermore, most of them – especially the theistic ones – have licensed and encouraged a ruthlessly anthropocentric exploitation of nature. But it is only fair to add that they can also act as significant repositories of human wisdom, and therefore resources with which to meet new (such as ecological) demands.[4] The point I want to emphasize, however, is that *religions do not exhaust the spiritual, or its importance.*[5] And that importance has direct relevance, both substantively and strategically, to an ecological ethic.

Negatively, as we have already seen, there is good reason to be suspicious of attempts to convince us that nature is strictly or merely 'natural'. Disenchanting the world, so that nature and its places and fellow inhabitants can no longer be seen as sacred, *is a fundamental prerequisite to commodifying and exploiting it.*[6] If you see nature as essentially a passive and inanimate object with no intrinsic value, you will feel free to do with it whatever you will, and you will. (That obviously includes, but is not limited to, the treatment of animals in factory farms and laboratories.) Nor will you feel sufficiently strongly moved to fight to protect it. In that case, a deep ecological ethic has no possible foothold. Indeed, for those who stand to profit from disenchantment, such an attitude and its corresponding ethic must be actively discouraged. The result in the not-so-long run, as Bateson remarked, is that if you see the world as simply yours to exploit '*and you have an advanced technology*', your likelihood of survival will be that of a snowball in hell' (1972: 462; italics in original).

Positively, the commitment to the intrinsic value of nature that is at the heart of a fully ecocentric ethic requires a recognition that its value cannot be exhausted by any use or understanding or even appreciation; it is more-than-human (although – needless, I hope, to add – that includes the human).[7] Such value is ultimately an inexhaustible mystery. It cannot be fully explained, analysed or justified in terms of other concepts or values; otherwise, it would not be intrinsic.

In other words, the source, the 'goal' and the practice of an eco-centric ethic are all, in this sense, spiritual. A post-secular – and indeed post-religious – spirituality[8] is therefore an inherent part of ecocentrism, and it is a part that no ecocentric movement can afford to do without. Nor is it by any means necessarily reactionary.

But in that case, what kind of spirituality? This is a key question. Tom Cheetham put it well:

> The call for a 'resacralization' of nature as a necessary condition for the solution of global and local environmental problems has much to recommend it insofar as it emphasizes the local, the timely, and the particular. Nevertheless, insofar as such a move grounds environmentalism in 'Nature' conceived as an alternative absolute, it is misguided and dangerous for all the reasons that such claims to transcendent knowledge always are. (1993: 309)

We have discussed the dangers of a conception of nature that is overly abstract, universal or 'transcendent', thus inviting an authoritarian politics. By the same token, monism is also dangerous. Exalting One True Nature (whether in mystical or scientific terms is ultimately secondary) or Gaian Earth or, for that matter, a single Earth-mother goddess leaves the logic of abstract monism – so hostile to nature as a pluralist, perspectival, sensuous experience – fundamentally untouched. I have also argued against any view of nature that tries to exclude humanity entirely (as distinct from opposing human chauvinism and allowing room for human/non-human conflicts). So Cheetham's warning is quite in order; but it does not exclude spirituality as such.

In addition, I have criticized another spirituality in relation to Deep Ecology, namely the privatized kind of the New Age consumer. Purely personal and private religious belief lends itself too easily to an anthropocentric egoism that is itself vulnerable to being co-opted by 'lifestyle' consumer capitalism.

The understanding of the sacred that can make a positive and effective contribution to ecocentric ethics, then, is a valuing of the Earth which is:

- *pluralist* (while allowing commonalities, with other people in other places also valuing nature in other ways, to emerge);
- *local* (while allowing connections with those others elsewhere);
- deeply appreciative of, and involved in, the so-called material world in all its *sensuous particulars*, and recognizes that being ultimately and fundamentally a mystery, it/they are not only or merely 'material'; and
- *social* as well as individual: if not exactly a religion, on account of the characteristics just mentioned, then a 'collective spirituality'.

The Land Ethic, Gaia Theory, Deep Ecology and Left Biocentrism all could contribute to and benefit from such a sense of the sacred, so different from the abstract universalism, both religious and secular, with which we are familiar. Ecofeminism too, in ways I have mentioned, has a potentially vital role in a pluralist, embodied and locally engaged ecological spirituality, or what Plumwood calls 'a materialist spirituality of place' (2002: ch. 10).

Another potent source of inspiration comes from aboriginal religions. Sean Kane writes: 'As civilization feels its way forward to practices of living with the earth on the earth's terms, we are discovering the respect for nature demonstrated by archaic humanity' (1994: 14). Now it is true that the way most surviving indigenous peoples live today is increasingly integrated into the global capitalist system, with the ecocidal consequences of its industrial dynamic; and no romanticism or cultural relativism should gloss over that fact. It is also true that the ancient aboriginal world included some ecological devastation (despite being hampered by the lack of modern technology).

Nonetheless, most indigenous peoples did manage, on balance, to coexist sustainably with the natural world considerably more successfully, and for a great deal longer, than moderns. And a key to their relative success has been an Earth-oriented spirituality with practical ethical implications which restrain, at least, destructive practices.[9] (It must be added, however, that another reason for their success, in addition to relatively low-impact technology, was simply much lower numbers; but this also was partly a result of the same ethic.)

For that reason, the recent popularity of debunking a strawman called 'the ecological Indian' is somewhat suspicious. In addition to being economical with the truth, it is too convenient for those who want to persuade us that *homo economicus* was, is and ever will be the sole master here.[10] As Anderson (1996) has convincingly shown, there are ecologies of the heart as well as mind, and they do make a real practical difference.

Furthermore, most of the attacks on aboriginal ecological 'balance' are unfair insofar as such stable systems are always *relatively*, not absolutely, stable. To quote Michael Novack:

> Most traditional societies were operationally stable in the environmental sense but usually lacked mechanisms to resist disturbance if faced with factors they did not co-evolve with. Thus a traditional American Indian hunting society might have had mechanisms in place that would prevent human unbalancing of the food animal species but no corresponding mechanism for animals just being killed for their skins; after all, how many skins could a semi-nomad carry around, how many were useful, and what sane person would waste time killing more fur-bearers than the fur of which they had use for? Bring outside fur-traders into the equation and the system collapses.

'The reality', he adds, 'is that this is not a fault which can be prevented. No matter what mechanisms are proposed to maintain stability and balance, it will always be possible to find some perturbation large enough or alien enough to upset the apple cart. . . . We can only hope our solution will not encounter what it is not designed to withstand.'[11] So to hold this against aboriginal 'solutions' is manifestly unfair, and indeed hypocritical.

What is needed is to encourage and strengthen people's awareness and appreciation – which already exists, although it is rarely articulated – of the Earth and all its life as sacred: not an abstract

Life, but one that is embodied and embedded in specific relation-ships, communities and places.[12] (There is a valid parallel here with what ecofeminists such as Salleh have pointed to: the nurturing labour, also already in place but too often unrecognized, that is a fundamental part of an effective ecocentrism.)

The best short term for such a spirituality is probably one which early anthropologists applied pejoratively to the religion of sup-posedly primitive people: *animism*.[13] But we need, and should, no longer accept their assumption of 'our' cultural superiority as Christians. As Kane writes, 'all the work that various peoples have done – all the work that peoples must do – to live with the Earth on the Earth's terms is pre-empted by the dream of transcendence' (1994: 255). That dream is as false as it is destructive.

# 10

## Moral Pluralism and Pragmatism

### The Poverty of Monism

Moral pluralism is the view that our ethical life consists of a number of different principles and values which can conflict, and which cannot be boiled down to just one. They can be compared practically in the course of arriving at a decision, but in themselves, to a greater or lesser extent, they are 'incommensurable', and any such decision, in taking one as its guide, always runs the risk of (so to speak) offending one or more of the others.

Such a view has been taken by some great thinkers: from Machiavelli and Nietzsche to William James, Max Weber and Isaiah Berlin.[1] In the latter's words:

> The notion that there must exist final objective answers to normative questions, truths that can be demonstrated or directly intuited, that it is in principle possible to discover a harmonious pattern in which all values are reconciled, and that it is towards this unique goal that we must make; that we can uncover some single central principle that shapes this vision, a principle which, once found, will govern our lives – this ancient and almost universal belief . . . seems to me invalid,

and at times to have led (and still to lead) to absurdities in theory and barbarous consequences in practice. (1969: lv–lvi)

Nonetheless, pluralism remains a distinctly minority view. The reason is simple, if deep: the dominant kind of ethics in the West – from Greek philosophical and Christian religious to modernist/ humanist – is profoundly monist. Its fundamental premise is that there is *a single reference point,* whereby, to quote Weber, 'one can, in principle, master all things by calculation' (1991: 139).[2] In terms of the logic of this belief, whether this single principle or value is spiritual (God) or material (scientific truth) is secondary, although not unimportant: the former, as the ultimate mystery, ultimately cannot be mastered, whereas the latter does hold out the promise of ultimate mastery. Such monism is necessarily also universalist, since if there is only one such principle it must, by definition, apply everywhere without exception. Of course, to ensure that the one truth is correctly perceived and promulgated, a cast of approved interpreters is also needed. The result, as Barbara Herrnstein Smith notes, is 'intellectual/political totalitarianism (the effort to identify the presumptively universally compelling Truth and Way and to compel it universally)' (1998: 179).

This worldview, and its operation, is one of the primary causes of our current ecological crisis, because, as Weber famously put it, the belief (note: *belief*) that everything can, at least in principle, be mastered by calculation results in 'the disenchantment of the world'. Now, as I mentioned earlier, the disenchantment of nature began with Greek philosophical monism (especially Plato) and monotheism, and in particular their combination in Christianity and later Islam. But it was sharply intensified by modern science. And we have seen that such disenchantment is a prerequisite to the physical desacration of nature by unrestrained exploitation.

It is also significant that it is virtually impossible to subscribe to a monist universalism without rejecting limits (since universal truth is, by definition, without any limits); and that rejection is another key element of anti-ecological modernity. Such monism is also deeply anthropocentric: it is humans alone who are licensed by God, or Truth, to work their will on nature without, in principle, any natural limits. Finally, it overrules our experience – perhaps particularly of nature – as worlds (plural) of effectively endless sensuous particulars.[3] In short, as William James demanded, 'Why should we envelop our many with the "one" that brings so much poison in its train?' (1977: 141).

Yet as we have also seen, any ecological fundamentalism would merely replace the one true and universal God with Nature. (It matters little whether the 'Nature' here is mystical or scientific.) Such a move would not only leave the destructive logic untouched, but ecocentrism, albeit of a pathological kind, would thereby become the enemy of nature. That would truly be a disaster.

It follows that the only way to resist and ultimately replace the inherently anti-ecological logic of monism is through pluralism. And that means a *moral* as well as epistemological pluralism.[4] To quote Weber again: 'We are placed into various life-spheres, each of which is governed by different laws.' And being different, 'the ultimately possible attitudes toward life are irreconcilable, and hence their struggle can never be brought to a final conclusion' (1991: 123, 152). Furthermore, as I have already argued, in this situation science cannot make ethical choices for us. It 'presupposes that what is yielded by scientific work is important in the sense that it is worth being known. . . . [But] this presupposition cannot be proved by scientific means. It can only be *interpreted* with reference to its ultimate meaning, which we must reject or accept according to our ultimate position towards life' (ibid. 143).

It follows that different considerations can *validly* apply in different cases, and that each case can *properly* be viewed in different ways.[5] Connections must then be made, and decisions taken, on grounds to be argued and established contingently in each case, which is to say (in the broad sense), politically. And those taking the decisions must therefore take responsibility for them, rather than hiding behind supposedly transcendental abstract truth.[6]

Abandoning what the philosopher Bernard Williams called 'a rationalistic conception of rationality' (1993: 18) – which asks reason (including scientific reason) to do what it cannot – does not make choice arbitrary, any more than does dispensing with the notion that truth must be singular. (There is a strong parallel here with what we saw earlier about how realists view the consequences of *what they think of* as relativism.) Neither confused nor dishonest, moral pluralism is, in Midgley's words, 'simply a recognition of the complexity of life'.[7]

Nor is it an ethical disaster. On the contrary, as Christopher Stone writes, 'It is by the choices we affirm in this zone of ultimate uncertainty that we have our highest opportunity to exercise our freedoms and define our characters' (1995: 525).[8] In other words, it is essential to the process of developing an ethically virtuous character – including ecologically virtuous – both individually and socially.[9]

## The Consequences of Pluralism

We began this book by noting the gravity of the current ecological crisis. The subject of moral pluralism provides an opportunity to ask: what follows from this crisis as such? The short and perhaps unwelcome answer is that nothing *necessarily* follows from it, no matter how serious it is or may become. The reason is that any perception, assertion, valuation and meaning of ecocrisis is unavoidably only one among others, none of which is self-evidently true, let alone their implications. All of them are unavoidably contingent (partial, local, unstable) – which is *not* to say merely subjective – and competing in a complex rhetorical economy of claims and counter-claims, values and counter-values, all of them with actual or potential winners and losers (relatively speaking, of course). As Smith puts it, 'There is no way to give a final reckoning that is simultaneously total and final. There is no Judgement Day. There is no *bottom* line anywhere, for anyone or for "man"' (1988: 149). Indeed, when the end of the world for human beings comes, the last two will probably be arguing about what it means (assuming, of course, that they notice in time). And if they aren't, the reason won't be because its meaning is obvious; it will be because they decided, and managed, to agree on something.

This is bound to be deeply frustrating for ecocentric ethicists. You can almost hear them saying, 'Everything – human rights, health, the lot – depends on ecosystems! No Earth, no nothing!' But I'm afraid that even this truth, unavoidably, is a claim and a value competing in that economy; and as such it is not, even so baldly put as that, self-evident. Nothing that could happen, not even severe ecosystemic breakdown or ecological collapse, would *in itself* make ecocentrism universally accepted; people would, and will, be able to come up with other explanations. ('God's will' is always popular.) So illusions of 'self-evident objective truths' only make the ecocentric work that needs to be done still harder. (We will look at that work in the following chapter.) In short, the upshot of a pluralist world for ecocentrism is an apparent paradox: eco-centrics realize that since everything on this Earth depends on it and its vital constituent parts – the true common good – *where human good, values or interests clearly conflict with the well-being of the Earth, the former must give way*; nonetheless, this realization cannot ever be taken for granted – as much as possible and wherever and whenever possible, *it must be argued, publicized, fought for and lived.*

There is a silver lining to this paradox, for pluralism helps relieve ecocentric ethicists of at least three burdens they are better off without:

1  A tendency to moral self-righteousness which is counter-productive in terms of its effect on members of the public whom they are trying to influence. However paradoxical it may seem, the intrinsic value of nature is something that must be estab-lished. And to proceed as if it was obvious (i.e., to everyone who isn't a fool or a knave) is not the most promising way to do so.

2  A tendency to despair when they dramatically fail to change the public and/or official mindset, *partly* because of the first problem, combined with underestimating just how hard it is to do so. Any positive change will be incremental, partial, uneven and contested, and a grasp of pluralism would make this clearer from the outset.

3  The potential, at least, to entertain a green version of 'intellec-tual/political totalitarianism', which in this case takes the form of dogmatic misanthropy. It is usually nothing more than a side effect of the personal despair just mentioned, which is a more serious occupational hazard for ecocentrics. Full-blooded and dangerous green misanthropy is actually strikingly rare, espe-cially compared with how common lethal anthropocentrism is.

The case for moral/ethical pluralism overlaps closely with that for **pragmatism**. That word commonly refers to a mindset primarily concerned with what works in practice as distinct from theory, and the philosophical version is not radically different; it simply fleshes out such concern theoretically and philosophically. Oversimplifying, practice, or *praxis*, in the relevant context, is both the starting point and terminus of theory, or what is considered to be true.[10]

The consequences for ecocentric ethics are practically identical with those of pluralism, with perhaps a slightly different emphasis. What follows is that ecocentrics must be able to work together with those who are committed to mid-green or intermediate, light green or shallow, and even outright anthropocentric, ethics when there is real potential common ground on a particular issue. An ecocentric point of view is one among many, not a revealed Truth, and allies are not exactly thick on the ground, so when the opportunity arises to do so without sacrificing ecocentric principles, alliances must be forged.

As Bryan Norton (1991) has pointed out, agreement on principles can *follow* agreement on practice, i.e., what to do in or about a concrete situation or problem. This is another aspect of the kind of labour-intensive, hands-on democracy-in-action just mentioned which ecocentric ethics requires in order to make a difference. Such agreement, however, is not a necessary 'principle'. There are absolutely no guarantees that policies in the interest of humanity and those in the interest of non-human nature will converge; all we can say is that they may.[11]

# 11

## Green Citizenship

### Making it Real

This book is not intended to offer a detailed analysis of the practical implementation of an ecocentric ethic. However, it would be irresponsible to say nothing about it whatsoever. So what would be required to make it one of the ethics, at least, that determines what actually happens – in short, an ethic with teeth?

As that question implies, an ecocentric ethic (I suggest) must be consequentialist; it must be able to make a real positive difference in the world. But it also must be deontological, inasmuch as it involves rules which are, through both rewards and punishments, actively enforced (encouraging a culture of encouraging ecocentric behaviour and shaming its opposite being at least as important as legal sanctions, although those too are needed). Finally and most crucially, however – as that last point also implies – realizing (i.e., making real) an ecocentric ethic is an instance of virtue ethics, of making ecological virtue a central value in our societies and cultures: in other words, encouraging *green citizenship*.

What does that work consist of? Broadly, the goal is to 'create and maintain structures and procedures that give as much scope as possible to the laborious working out, individually and in concert, of courses of action that are the "best" (all things considered . . .) for each, and each set, of us' (Smith 1988: 179). Less abstractly, there are educational, political, economic, social and cultural dimensions to green citizenship, all of which are important.

For example, deep ecological ethics must be brought to the attention of both the relevant authorities and the public, although not in the same way, of course. Authorities must be helped to reconceptualize their perceived political and economic remits in relation to the ecological dimension; the public, to imagine plausible cultural and social life-narratives which include that dimension. Somewhere in between, sharing both these challenges, are the community decision-makers.

For many people and organizations directly involved with ecological ethics, the primary task is to get ecocentric ideas and values into the 'collective mindstream' of the NGOs, think-tanks, quasi-academic institutes and the media, which tend to determine what become 'issues' and how they are treated, and which are themselves trying to influence state/government policy regarding these issues. This can be more productive and important than lobbying the government ('up one level') directly, although of course that too is often necessary. Doing so will often involve articulating and construing the concerns and fears of so-called ordinary people ('down one level'), though again, not just doing that. Getting an idea 'onto the table' is often a prerequisite for getting it to influence action – whether action by the state or in some grass-roots way.[1]

The work that needs doing also includes patient and dogged efforts to influence the institutions – e.g., all the media, schools and universities – that in turn tend to control how people perceive natural goods.[2] (Textbooks and monographs certainly have their place in this process; on the other hand, a few 'green' popular TV soap operas would probably do more to propagate ecocentric values, and faster, than any number of specialist books could do in the time-frame that the urgency of the ecological situation dictates.)

For the great majority of people, it must be said, the survival of biodiversity, or even of the human species as such, is so abstract as to be virtually meaningless. But this is just the sort of thing that requires cultural as well as political work, creative as much as intellectual or political, enabling it to become real in our collective imagination.

One of the problems here is that to the extent an ethic remains fundamentally conventional (anthropocentric), it will tend to be persuasive but effect little change; whereas to the extent it is radical (ecocentric), it will tend, for that very reason, to be easily marginalized. As Andrew McLaughlin observes: 'A radical critique that questions society's basic belief system and also wishes to gain assent from the members of that society must confront the fact that any appeal to "common sense" or intuitions will not go deeply enough because our common sense is part of the problem' (1993: 170).

A related point is that an appeal *purely* to ecocentric altruism seems in general almost certainly bound to fail. Yet an appeal to 'enlightened' self-interest is highly vulnerable to people's selfishness, short sense of time-scale, and narrow interpretations of 'self', e.g., myself and my family, now and maybe for the next few years – all of which invites more ecological destruction. There is no escaping these general dilemmas, and every actual situation will require a different mix and balance, a compromise with reference to its particular problem and context.

Of course, if an ecocentrically radical politics is sufficiently pragmatic, and an anthropocentrically reformist politics is sufficiently extensive, they meet, rendering the distinction irrelevant in practice. It is also true that 'we do not in all cases need to await agreement on principles (much less on social solutions in which they are applied) before particular problems can be recognized as such' (Attfield 1983: 7).[3] However – and this is the key point – the ecocrisis requires an ecocentric ethic as a *regulative horizon*, an ethical context and ideal which may never be fully attained but nonetheless indicate the right direction and help move things that way. As F. M. Alexander remarked, 'There is no such thing as a right position, but there is a right direction' (2000: 73).

## A Long Revolution?

As Sylvan and Bennett (among others) have remarked, real change can come about in two basic ways – and there are serious problems with both. One is slowly, through *reform*. But 'the overwhelming evidence is that not nearly enough will happen in time for anything but a grossly impoverished natural environment to emerge. . . . For much of the world's remaining wildernesses, for most of its remaining species, it is going to be all over in the next 20 years or so' (1994: 218–19). Reform virtually never happens with that sort of speed, especially when the initial odds are so heavily against it. The alternative is *revolution*, at least in a few key states. But 'were the styles of historic revolutions emulated, it would be a problematic and likely nasty medicine' (ibid.). Such a revolution – for which it seems there would be little public support anyway – is very hard to achieve satisfactorily, and there is always the possibility that a state could 'fall the wrong way, for instance to a totalitarian far right' (ibid.). Of course, public opinion and political conditions could change if something goes badly wrong. And as Herman Daly says, it may well take 'a Great Ecological Spasm to convince people that something is wrong with an economic theory that denies the very possibility of an economy exceeding its optimal scale. But even in that unhappy event, it is still necessary to have an alternative vision ready to present when crisis conditions provide a receptive public' (quoted in McLaughlin 1993: 218).

Would there be ready and available, in that case, sufficiently well-thought-out and detailed ecocentric alternatives? Sylvan and Bennett wisely conclude that 'Requisite organization, well-thought-through directions, plans for action, and restructuring: such features are critical. Deep environmental groups should begin to prepare, carefully and thoroughly' (1994: 120). But equally important is the attitude suggested by Jones, to be a practical idealist: 'one who is accepting of her fear (and there is plenty to be afraid of) without being possessed by it. Living beyond optimism and pessimism, she is a patient and clear-sighted *possibilist*' (1993: 190).

Indeed, the question of attitude should not be neglected in a rush to green activism. It is to the credit of the green movement – including its 'spiritual' wing, neo-paganism – that compared to the New Age movement and new religious movements, there is less self-indulgent spirituality in which the 'external' or 'outer' world, including nature, is regarded as secondary or inferior. (To see nature in such a way simply accepts the premise of modern science of a nature without significant agency, subjectivity or soul.) But that does not mean that questions of one's own personal and subjective involvement with ecocentrism are entirely optional. Their complete neglect can result not only in losing touch with what one is trying to defend, but in 'burn-out' and despair that puts an end to activism too.[4]

Of course, the need for change is urgent; biotechnology, global warming, overpopulation, deforestation, extinctions and too many other crises will not, in a real sense, wait. But a longer view too is necessary, and much of it has to do with encouraging practices embodying the ethical virtue of green citizenship. It could be said, without much exaggeration, that it is only in the light of an eco-centric ethic that humans causing these things can be perceived as acting wrongly, even criminally; and it is only by the public expression of such an ethic through active green citizenship that anything will be done about them. Transnational companies are unlikely to forgo huge profits unbidden, any more than governments are to vote themselves out of office for a poor environmental record. 'A steady-state economy', as Jones points out, 'cannot exist without a whole steady-state culture to support it' (ibid. 115). Further to that point, there is, for example, an urgent need for 'ecoliteracy' (Capra 1997: 289–95). It should, and easily could, be a fundamental part of every child's education to learn where his or her water, energy, food, etc. come from (and wastes go to), and with what other effects.

## Ecological Republicanism

While on the subject of the people, however, let us also dispense with the notion, which some greens have inherited from anarchism, that left to themselves (whatever that may mean), human beings will just naturally 'do the right thing'; or that human life, beyond a very small population indeed, is possible without social and political structures. The evidence in support of either idea is in short supply. Nor can such structures ever be purely emancipatory: that about them which enables is also, in different ways and/or for different people, what unavoidably constrains. (Contrariwise, as Foucault recognized, nor are they ever purely repressive; at the very least, they create new patterns of resistance.)

As Adrian Oldfield remarks, 'The moral character which is appropriate for genuine citizenship does not generate itself; it has to be authoritatively inculcated' (1990: 164).[5] Certainly 'authoritative' should not be 'authoritarian', and need not be. But to expect it to work without duties as well as rights, punishments as well as rewards, losers as well as winners, is indefensibly naive; these will unavoidably figure strongly in any green citizenship worth the name. (They do so *already*, of course, in its absence; but for very different ends, virtually all of them highly anthropocentric.) In some cases, what is required may well take the form, in Hardin's words, of 'mutual coercion, mutually agreed upon by the majority of people affected' (in Benson 2000: 194) – although if so agreed, does it then remain 'coercion'? (Again, it is quite absurd to pretend that we are presently not subjected to any coercion, whether directly or indirectly.)

There is much to learn here from the tradition of civic republicanism[6] – probably more than from its modern, and more timid cousin, communitarianism.[7] It is also significant that virtue ethics is closely related to, probably inseparable from, that tradition. And virtue ethics is the right context for setting a new or renewed framework for humanity *within* nature, especially for determining what counts as ordinary and acceptable behaviour. (Historically, in contrast, utilitarianism has been vital to reform movements, generating 'patches' where they were most needed, and deontological ethics has been useful in maintaining a balance between the rights of the individual and of society.)

But ecofeminists are also right to emphasize practices of caring and nurturing, which have a vital contribution to make – in this case, negatively, by helping to prevent an ecological republicanism from degenerating into yet another masculinist programme (only this time in the name of the Earth), and positively, by reminding us that a great deal of the kind of attitude that is needed already exists as the unrecognized and undervalued work of (overwhelmingly) women.[8]

It is a tall order: to combine republican toughness and ecofeminist tenderness, so to speak – although both also contain the contrary virtues in their way (the dream of a self-governing citizenry, and feminine realism) – in a green virtue ethics for the twenty-first century. But the situation we are in demands no less. And it is significant, and hopeful, that they share a fundamental concept, and value, that has been lost in the modernist worship of Progress: the common good. Only now, it must be an *ecological common good*, that of all the communities that make up the republic of life on Earth.[9]

There should be no illusions about establishing a green utopia, however. In addition to obvious political dangers, as Callicott says, 'An ethic is never [fully] realized on a collective social scale and only very rarely on an individual scale. . . . An ethic constitutes, rather, an ideal of human behaviour . . . [but] it nonetheless exerts a very real force on practice' (1994: 2–3). A powerfully ecocentric version of such an ethic, where there is now effectively almost none, would help get us closer, at least, to heaven on Earth – which is where we most need it.

## A Note on Cunning Wisdom

It hardly needs stressing that the project of green virtue, or ecocentric citizenship, faces many serious difficulties. It will require both political and emotional intelligence, will and (not least) luck. It has many enemies, in both high and low places, and, as Machiavelli pointed out, 'The fact is that a man who wants to act virtuously *in every way* necessarily comes to grief among so many who are not virtuous' (1981: 91; my italics). Furthermore, as I have said, living in a plural world means that values sometimes conflict, with no ideal or painless resolution. Taking these points together, it follows that although it is both ethically and strategically important for ecocentric activists to accommodate as many different virtuous ideals as possible, it will rarely be possible to accommodate them all.

There is no single blueprint for how to act, no set of infallible rules or guidelines; but act we must. (Doing nothing is, of course, just another kind of action.) Yet although the extent of our present ecocrisis is unprecedented, such uncertainty is not, and negotiating it is inherent in being alive. For that reason, cultural traditions have some advice to offer here. For example, Christ advised us to be not only harmless as doves, but wise as serpents (Matthew 10: 16). Buddhism emphasizes the inseparability of compassion for suffering on the one hand and *upaya*, or 'skilful means', on the other. Aristotle stressed the value of *phronesis*, or practical (as distinct from theoretical) wisdom, and the still more ancient Greek term *metis* implies the same as Chinese *zhi*, namely wisdom as cunning.[10] Machiavelli emphasized the same thing: the need to be *able* to act wrongly (in relation to one principle) in order to act virtuously in relation to what one judges to be more important in the present situation. (He did not assert that that 'justifies' the action, however; it remains morally wrong.)

Another unlikely agreement may also be significant: both the Chinese Neo-Confucians and Montaigne, their approximate contemporary and perhaps the most influential European humanist, concurred that one cannot be fully human if one's concern is only for humans; in other words, without being *humane*.[11] Is it a coincidence that they were pre-modern (and the former non-Western), before the time where we learned to overrule our ancient kinship with all life in favour of our own kind alone? In any case, Chu Hsi (1130–1200) influentially defined *jen*, or humanity, as 'the feeling of love, respect, being right, and discrimination between right and wrong – and the feeling of commiseration pervades them all' (Chan 1963: 594). There was, quite deliberately, no attempt to stipulate a restricted class of appropriate *objects* of commiseration. The source of *jen* was life itself, and so too, in all its manifestations, was its appropriate object. Similarly, Montaigne (1533–92) reflected that:

> There is a kind of respect and a duty in man as a genus which link us not merely to the beats, which have life and feelings, but even to trees and plants. We owe justice to men; and to the other creatures who are able to receive them we owe gentleness and kindness. Between them and us there is some sort of intercourse and a degree of mutual obligation. (1991: 488)[12]

Without compassion – for fellow human beings, certainly, but for the rest of life no less – we would not care about the ecological holocaust, and there would be nothing more to discuss. But without intelligence, wisdom and sometimes even cunning, we shall not get very far in stopping it, nor in bringing about something better.

# 12

# *A Case-Study: Human Overpopulation*

## The Problem

We have already touched on human population as a factor in the $I = PLOT$ equation. Now at 6.3 billion, it has doubled since the 1960s and is expected to reach about 9 billion by the middle of this century. But out of all the possible ecological problems, why choose population as an example? Because it is a kind of test case for ecocentrism. Population is significantly different from factors of the dynamic of ecocide because unlike, say, consumption or technology, it directly involves – indeed, in a sense, *is* – human beings as such, and therefore an ecocentric challenge.

More precisely, in order to recognize it *as* a genuine problem, you have to be able to challenge a fundamentally anthropocentric assumption which, although rarely articulated, amounts to a gut feeling that 'Of course, human beings are good – indeed, the highest good – so the more human beings, the better!' And conversely, 'Anyone who wants to see fewer human beings here must hate them!'

Now a moment's thought will show that these two statements are deeply flawed, and that the conclusions don't necessarily follow at all from their premises even if those are granted:

- Are humans always and everywhere a good (let alone the highest good)?
- A good rarely increases arithmetically without any limits past which it stops being a good and becomes a problem (think of the consumption of food, for example). Why should collective human good be a quantitative, indeed additive, phenomenon?
- Two of the towering cultural peaks of all human history, by most reckonings, occurred in Athens of the fourth–fifth century BCE and Florence of the fifteenth–sixteenth century CE – where the population was no higher than the tens and hundreds of thousands respectively: a tiny percentage of our current population. (The same general point could be made of another candidate, Sung dynasty China.)
- It is perfectly possible to want there to be fewer new people because you fear for those who already exist. To quote the present Dalai Lama, 'There are six billion precious lives on Earth. All of them are under direct threat from other precious lives that are being added by the million.'[1]
- What about the individuals, places and species that are the victims of mass extinction as a direct result of human beings continually taking and making over new territory?

But when it comes to thinking about and discussing human population, we are not usually dealing with logic, concepts or evidence so much as a *mentality*, and one which embodies a deeply defended anthropocentrism. Thus, even many otherwise enlightened and progressive individuals, who have no trouble in arguing for lower levels of consumption and green technologies, bitterly resist looking human population – and all the more so, the present *over*population – in the face. The result is what Irvine (2002) calls the 'overpopulation denial syndrome' (ODS):[2] a disgraceful silence on this subject, enforced by the fear of being accused of misanthropy, authoritarianism, racism or sexism, as a result of which anyone who does raise it is almost automatically accused of one or more of those unpleasant things. (The charge of racism is especially potent.)

This silence often involves an unholy alliance of political left and right. For the *right*, when religious, 'overpopulation' represents an intolerable threat to dogma of the sanctity of individual human life, no matter in what conditions; when non-religious, the threat is to the secular cult of humanism.[3] For the *left*, which shares a good deal of ground with the previous position, just to raise the issue of over-population is evidence of hatred of humanity, or people of colour, or women. It seems to make no difference when the point is also made that since a child born in Britain, say, will put 30–40 times more strain on global resources than one born in Bangladesh, pop-ulation control is probably most urgent in the overdeveloped world.

Even non-governmental organizations (NGOs) tiptoe around the P-word, addressing it, if at all, as a mere side effect of another supposedly more basic and politically acceptable problem, such as poverty, women's lack of education and access to reproductive health facilities and health care, etc. We shall review these points in a moment; they are certainly all valid and urgent concerns, but they do not remove the need to recognize population as a fundamental and pressing dynamic *in itself*. Note too that these are *all* anthro-pocentric concerns; but even within that ambit, as McLaughlin notes, 'Combining social justice with an increasing population is like running down the up escalator. Increasing effort is required just to stay in place' (1993: 216).

It is true that no single one of the PLOT factors (population, lifestyle or consumption, organization and technology) offers a complete solution to ecological crisis. In all major human-caused ecological problems, more than one is implicated and needs addressing: 'both-and', not 'either-or'. Nor are all ecological prob-lems the direct result of overpopulation; in particular, if the overde-velopment and overconsumption powered by global corporate capitalism continues unabated, their effects will need no help from other quarters. Nonetheless, it does not require genius to realize that if human population continues to grow at a sufficient rate for long enough, then no amount of technological tweaking (always assuming it is politically feasible) or reduction of consumption (which, at the moment, is certainly *not* politically feasible) will suffice to control and then reduce our ecological impact.

In addition, overpopulation has the peculiarly vicious result that simply by force of numbers, the most *natural* human activities, relat-ing most directly to survival and the continuation of the species – finding fuel, shelter, growing food, procreation, excretion and so on – themselves become pathological: direct threats to personal survival and to that of the species, plus other lives and species.

## Analysing Overpopulation

This is the context in which world population has now reached 6.3 billion, and is still rising. Despite much recent publicity about a trend 'reversed', what has started to decline (with no guarantees that it will continue) is the rate of increase; but the number of people is still growing, *and it is already far too high*. To quote Ward Churchill, the American Indian Movement leader:

> Any serious discussion of global problem resolution must begin with the observation that a 5.25 billion human population [as it then was] is in itself outrageously unrealistic. The question then becomes not how we sustain such a ludicrous overburden of one species, but how we begin to inculcate a broad consciousness leading to the steady scaling back of human numbers to some point well below 50% of the present level, and keep it there. (Quoted in McCormick 1994: 6–7)

Why is it too high? There are powerful reasons, both anthropocentric, concerning purely human well-being, and ecocentric, directly affecting the survival of most other animal species too, along with any remaining wilderness. In the earlier section on ecocrisis, we touched on the dimensions of that crisis in terms of biodiversity, habitat loss, species extinction, climate change and pollution.[4] Overpopulation has a direct hand in all of these. Other perspectives point to the same conclusion.

First, human use of biological resources overall currently far exceeds the rate at which they can renew themselves. Furthermore, using up this natural 'capital' probably contributes to a reduction in the rate of replenishment itself, which means that any overshoot is especially dangerous even though it is not immediately obvious what is going on.[5] Yet the present (early 2000s) overshoot of 20 per cent is projected to increase to between 80 and 120 per cent by 2050.[6]

Second, in 1999, there were only about 2.2 hectares of ecologically productive land per person on Earth. When (much more likely than 'if') the population grows to 9 billion, that figure will come down to 1.5 – hardly enough to provide everyone with a good diet, never mind sustainably supply energy requirements, etc. And third, some ecologists have suggested that in order to attain long-term viability and sustainability, as much as 50 per cent of the Earth's major ecosystems need to be either retained or restored; others, to the same end, have envisaged one-third natural, one-third small settlements and low-impact agriculture and one-third urban. In either case, a major reduction in population would be required.[7]

At this point, I need to introduce some concepts, most of them quite recent, which are very important to understanding population and its ecological impact.[8] *Pherology* is 'the science of the human carrying-capacity of the Earth or specific parts of the Earth'. The term was coined by Alec Ponton.[9] There are now a number of (small) organizations involved in this study, under the umbrella of the European Pherology Organizations Confederation (EPOC).

*Carrying capacity* is: 'The estimated human impact which a defined zone of the Earth can sustain over a given timescale without long-term degradation.' It is determined by the amount of renewable resources available and the amount of waste that can be assimilated by natural processes without resulting in long-term deterioration of the ecosystem (ibid.). The most important single criterion for establishing human carrying capacity is the amount of ecologically productive land. And that amount, to state the obvious, is limited. Technophiles believe that can be overcome through increased agricultural efficiency. Certain questions, however, remain conspicuously unanswered, starting from the fact that when (again, not 'if') the decline of global oil production starts to impact on fertilizer production, the productivity of the industrial agriculture that supports otherwise unsustainable population growth will start to fall dramatically.[10] But even if this were *not* the case, do they believe present levels could continue indefinitely? With no effects that undermine the ecological base? And with no other significant costs, such as impact on human and/or environmental health, other species and ecosystems?

*Ecological footprint* is 'the total area of productive land and water required on a continuous basis to produce all the resources consumed, and to assimilate all the wastes produced, by that population, wherever on Earth that land is located' (Wackernagel and Rees 1996).[11] The concept originated with William Rees (1992). When demand in a particular area, such as a country, exceeds supply – as it now frequently does – the ecological deficit is made up by appropriating the produce of land elsewhere. So the ecological footprint of a country such as the Netherlands or the UK, for example, vastly exceeds its geographical size. (That deficit could be reduced either by reducing per capita consumption and/or reducing the number of consumers.)

These concepts are interrelated, of course. For example, Rees has estimated that humanity's current ecological footprint already exceeds the entire Earth's long-term carrying capacity by as much as 40 per cent (2002: 40). It also becomes possible to ask some very pertinent if uncomfortable questions:

1   Is it ethically defensible for the ecological footprint of a country or region to exceed its own borders, and, if so, under what circumstances? Does this happen voluntarily, and if so is the recompense for those elsewhere who are supporting it (since we can assume they are not doing so as an act of charity) fair and just?

2   Relatedly, is it ethically defensible to encourage ideas, values and/or activities that collectively entail exceeding the carrying capacity of the Earth as a whole? That, of course, is just what the current world economic system does, with its unsustainably polluting and high-energy technologies; but the same question applies to encouraging large families.

3   Allowing (as one always must) for the limits of our present knowledge, what is the global population optimum, especially in relation to the planet's carrying capacity? Part of what is required to answer this question is some agreement as to what constitutes an acceptable level of consumption – 'acceptable' both ethically (e.g., reasonably equal everywhere) and practico-politically, so that those with the power to decide find it preferable (to put it bluntly) to simply killing off masses of others.

4  Relatedly, how many people do we arguably need, or are desirable, as opposed to how many can we squeeze onto the planet? Sheer numbers are certainly no guarantee of creativity or happiness, as I have suggested. But the prerequisite for all other human interests is ecological health. John Ruskin, that prophet without honour, was right: 'THERE IS NO WEALTH BUT LIFE'[12] – *all* life (1998: 270).

It turns out that the most closely reasoned estimates for a human population for the Earth that is within its total carrying capacity – allowing for an average 'European' standard of living for all (although with reduced or more efficient energy consumption), sustainable use of natural resources, and some remaining wild places – agree that it is a maximum of *around 2 billion people*.[13] Indeed, Mosquin and Rowe of the Manifesto for Earth arrive at the figure of the global population when it was last sustainably within the planet's overall carrying capacity, roughly at the beginning of the Industrial Revolution: one-sixth of its present number, or *1 billion*.[14]

Of course, this point has more local versions. For example, the UK's population – already high, still rising, and with ongoing immigration – is about 60 million. Its ecological footprint thus greatly exceeds its own area. Furthermore, as Optimum Population Trust (OPT) researcher Andrew Ferguson points out, it is only by 'extravagent use of fossil fuel' that even the present number can be supported, and that is starting to run out; he estimates a sustainable figure to be, at most, 30 million. Yet Britain's runaway number of teenage pregnancies (40,000 a year, far ahead of the nearest European country) attracts little policy attention, and calls to rethink immigration are associated firmly with the far right. 'Genuine asylum seekers and others reasonably admitted can be black, khaki, purple or green', argues OPT co-chair John Guillebaud, 'as long as we bring immigration and emigration into balance and control teenage pregnancies over five to six generations. . . . That could bring the UK to 30 million by 2130.'[15] Yet this is a generous timeframe, and there is very little evidence of either joined-up governmental thinking or informed public concern. And this national example could be multiplied many times over.

## What Overpopulation Is and Is Not

At this point, let us review the most common objections to taking overpopulation seriously, as opposed to viewing it as not very important and/or as a mere function of something else.[16]

'The population explosion is over.' This ignores the fact of *population momentum*, which means that total numbers will keep on rising long after a fall in the rate of increase. 'With regard to the long-term stability of the world's ecosystems and our ability to feed everyone adequately and to give them a reasonably good life, that margin of 3 or 4 billion extra people could be critical' (John Caldwell, quoted in Kates 2004: 52–3).

'Affluence is the answer', also known as the 'Demographic Transition Theory', according to which a country's birth rate will fall when it achieves sufficient wealth. The USA alone, whose burgeoning population (from births as well as immigration) does not exactly manifest sub-replacement fertility, exposes this fallacy.

'Affluence is the problem' or 'Poverty is the problem.' (A corollary is 'Only rich countries are the problem.') But huge numbers of the not-so-affluent also have an impact. Even with very low levels of consumption, sheer numbers can turn a once-sustainable practice, such as slash-and-burn cultivation, into a devastating one. 'Granted the rich are more destructive than the poor, but the poor too require shelter, clothing and food that has to come from somewhere on Earth. They've got an ecological footprint too. The numbers matter' (Stan Rowe, personal communication). Furthermore, raising the poor out of poverty (currently about 1.3 billion people, with millions more arriving every month) will unavoidably increase per capita pollution and consumption. And this is something a progressive agenda cannot *not* support. In addition, citizens of the rich 'North' have a much higher impact through consumption and technology, but immigrants soon adopt the same patterns. The consequence of immigration is therefore significantly to increase ecological impact, while the resulting population reduction in their country of origin is tiny. (Remember, the Earth is completely non-discriminatory. If two persons' impact is identical, their class, race and gender is, in this context, irrelevant.)

Finally, almost no one seems to have considered the possibility that 'population stabilisation and then reduction (by whatever humane and just means are appropriate to each situation) could actually be *precursor* to the take-off out of poverty' (Stevens 2003).

'Reproductive and sexual healthcare and family planning are the answer.' It *is* scandalous that more than one-third of all couples worldwide do not have access to proper contraception, and equally so that about 600,000 women every year die preventable deaths in pregnancy and childbirth (roughly the equivalent of four fully loaded jumbo jets crashing every day).[17] These are ethical issues in their own right, and contraception is certainly a vital part of reducing population. The implications for overpopulation, however, are not necessarily straightforward (see the following point).

'Female empowerment, especially education, is the answer.' Again, this is desirable in itself, and in most situations probably helps to reduce the number of births. But the work of Virginia Abernethy has shown that there is no simple connection, and certainly no necessary one, between increasing prosperity, health care and the education of women and fewer children. These do have positive effects but they can be overruled by the fact that, ultimately, 'people have as many children as they think can be raised well, according to their own standards'. So a sense of expanding opportunities can easily lead to larger families, and of shrinking ones to smaller.[18]

'There are enough resources to go around if properly distributed', or (even more wishfully mantra-like), 'Always enough for need, never enough for greed'. But in addition to the points above concerning affluence/poverty, sooner or later, if unchecked, ongoing expansion of population and/or consumption will catch up with *any* redistribution of a finite cake.

'Increasing food production alone can cure world hunger.' This assumes that present levels of production will continue or even increase, despite worsening soil impoverishment and depletion, aquifer exhaustion, chemical contamination, etc., not to mention (human-induced) climate change (see the questions raised earlier about agricultural innovation), and countenances turning over virtually all remaining wilderness with any agricultural potential to cultivation. Even more implausibly, it assumes that overpopulation will somehow take care of itself (humanely, of course). Without any steps to control population, it thus locks humanity further into the zero-sum dynamic of more food, leading to more births, requiring more food, requiring more industrialization of food production, resulting in more births . . . Pointing to the achievements of the 'Green Revolution' (and ignoring their costs), advocates now promise new miracles from biotechnology. But there is no exit strategy from the tightening spiral (or at least, no humane one), for which *collective addiction* would seem to provide the best model. This position is the height of ethical irresponsibility, especially when it comes from those who are offering, for a handsome profit, to supply the fix.[19]

'We need more workers and production.' But to quote Kenneth Boulding, 'Anyone who believes exponential growth can go on forever in a finite world is either a madman or an economist.'[20]

'We don't need to reduce population because environmental problems can be solved by technological means.' But all technologies have an environmental impact, and despite endless promises, there are limits on how clean *and* affordable they can become. More people with the same overall per capita consumption will therefore inevitably cancel out gains from more efficient and less polluting technologies.

'We need more young people to look after old people.' But, 'If we all have more children in order to look after more old people, you only have to wait for 70 years and you will have even more old people to look after.'[21] And if those young people are to be supplied by immigration, is it ethical, or even simply intelligent, for nations with lower birth rates to be asked to absorb large excess populations from those with high rates? Surely the latter should be encouraged (and helped) to act responsibly and control their own birth rates, rather than exporting the problem in a finite world.[22] Equally, 'developed' countries should try to assist them (always assuming local governments are trying too) to improve the conditions that induce emigration. And in any case, local people cannot fairly be asked to bear fewer children if at the same time you ask them to accept the immigration of others not making the same sacrifice, which will defeat the effect of any such sacrifice.[23] The overall level of consumption increases, of course, with the introduction of every additional person. But the overdeveloped world engages in disproportionately high consumption. Unless the countries of origin can succeed in lowering their birth rates, therefore, immigration to countries where consumption levels are already high further increases the net strain upon the Earth without even significantly relieving the countries of origin, where those leaving are quickly replaced.

'Reproductive rights are a non-negotiable freedom.'[24] But are they unaccompanied by any corresponding duty? Is *any* right? The civic republican and communitarian traditions, at least, suggest not.[25] The ethically unacceptable impacts of human overpopulation point firmly to the conclusion that now, 'All of the world's peoples must come fully to terms with the fact that a person's (biological) right to have children must be mediated by his or her (social) responsibility not to have too many' (Smail 1997: 189). I might add that anyone who nonetheless insists on reproduction as their absolute right or freedom, thus denying that they have any limits or duties in regard to that right, might reflect that they are inviting a corresponding denial from others that *they* have any duty to feed or support those children.[26]

Of course, just as a steady-state economy requires a steady-state culture to support it, that responsibility will require a small-family culture. But it will not happen without political leadership too, and regulatory measures encouraging population control *as such*. In addition to encouraging female education, family planning and widespread access to birth control, these should include such measures as removing government subsidies for children after the second, and perhaps recovering the social and ecological costs of such further children through taxation. As Norman Myers says:

> Of course two children are every couple's right. It is their right too to have a third child without asking anybody's approval. But everybody else has a right to ask the couple to pay the additional costs entrained for everybody else by that third child. These are costs the child will impose upon everybody's environment and hence on everybody's economy. (1998)

Recovering some of these public costs through taxation is possible. But that would depend on a wider and deeper realization that it no longer makes sense to allow parents the 'right to procreate as much as they please, while in doing so they restrict everybody else's right to live as they please' (ibid.).

The 'right' to have any number of children (and now at almost any age, with expensive medical assistance) is widely upheld. Similarly, as noted earlier, advocates of measures to control population – humane and sensible measures, not forced sterilizations or eugenics – are often accused of misanthropy, while those who make the charge implicitly lay claim to compassion (within a strictly human context). Couples who have decided not to bear children are still widely regarded as odd, at best.[27] But what if some restraint now for some people means a better quality of life for more people in the not-so-distant future? And what if indulgence today means drastically greater hardship and suffering tomorrow? What if 'natal authoritarianism' results in more future liberty, whereas the actions (and non-action) of 'liberals' now ends in greater repression? The ecological evidence strongly suggests that population planning, as Jack Parsons writes, 'is not an invasion of liberty but a safeguard of liberty. . . . The key question is not "Would population control reduce individual liberty?" but "Would population control reduce individual liberty more than unrestricted population growth?"' (1997: 5).[28]

## Overpopulation and Ecocentrism

The upshot of the discussion so far is the need for a decent, but urgent, reduction of human population as soon as possible.[29] But unlike the rest of this book, it argues that case mostly on anthropocentric grounds. We have had to do so because Overpopulation Denial Syndrome has so obscured the whole subject, even from the viewpoint of human self-interest, together with the disastrous consequences of overpopulation for non-human nature. It is now time to clarify some of those.

The basics should be fairly obvious. Humanity has already taken over at least a quarter of the planet's natural energy, two-thirds of its habitable land surface and 50 per cent of its fresh run-off water. The result is energy, room and water that is ever-increasingly *not* available to all other species which are not directly or indirectly sub-servient to our needs and wants. So much for the wild! And this is a process which the demands resulting from sheer numbers – at least as much as consumption and technology – are causing to acceler-ate all the time.

In addition to the shallow or light green reasons there is also a powerful intermediate or mid-green case for population control, in two respects:

1 Colonizing ever more land for ever more human beings, for shelter, food and fuel, involves killing off its aboriginal non-human inhabitants, so to speak, and taking away their land. The present rate of extinctions is already ample evidence, although what they fail to communicate is the brutality of the slaughter, the shame on us, and the tragedy of the loss. In the words of Alice Walker:

> Part of what justice means for non-human animals is that there will just have to be fewer people, because I think the insistence of people on covering the Earth itself is a grievous insult to the non-human animals whose space is squeezed into nonexistence. Just because people can have three, four and five children does not mean that that's best for all creation. It definitely is not. (Quoted in McCormick 1994: 6–7)

2 Ever more human beings, demanding ever more cheap (but healthy) food, are causing immense suffering for billions of intelligent social animals in 'efficient' factory farms, along with millions in laboratories so they can have 'safe' medicines, cos-metics, etc. That such suffering is *unnecessary* – in a manner, and on a scale, that is not true for a subsistence hunter where there are few alternatives – is the strongest possible ethical case for reducing and arguably rejecting medical experimentation on animals, and for not eating meat produced by factory farms.

Finally, there is deep or dark green case. This is at once the most urgent one and the hardest to argue. Urgent because (as the Earth Manifesto, in particular, makes clear) what is ultimately at stake –

nature itself – is the source of *all* value, human and non-human alike. Hard, because, overwhelmingly, people are unaware of their utter eco-dependence.

Gaia Theory implies that the Earth as such will survive our depradations nicely, thank you. But in addition to this providing rather cold comfort, consider the post-human New World. The odds are high, especially if (human-caused) climate change is the primary factor, that we would take most of the planet's remaining complex life-forms with us, or those still left, and render it uninhabitable for the foreseeable future by any possible heirs. Will anyone argue that this is ethically admirable or even defensible behaviour, even as a risk?

Here too, the statistics cannot do justice to the ethical obscenity of (say) an old-growth forest – literally irreplacable, biotically rich beyond our comprehension, and home to countless non-human lives – devastated and converted into telephone directories, plywood shuttering, mail-order sales catalogues and toilet-paper, not to mention cattle-feed in order to supply hamburgers. Other examples are possible, of course, but as a matter of fact, most of the new land continually being appropriated to meet the demands of ever more humans and to make up for cropland lost to urbanization and degradation (yet another function of overpopulation) comes from forests.[30]

This is also where the limitations of the anthropocentric case are most apparent. The argument above for taxing large families, for example, assumes that all significant effects on the environment of overpopulation are costable economically. But it is a fallacy to assume that all value can be converted into a single financial calculus; indeed, it is one of the most ecologically destructive beliefs today. As Paul Erhlich has remarked, 'The economy is a wholly-owned subsidiary of the Earth's ecology', and it is so in ways that far outrun any possible full financial or fiscal accountancy. Similarly, my criticisms of an unrestricted right to bear children were all limited to its effects on other people. But the effects on the natural world are at least as dire. Meanwhile, the entire debate about rights is about purely *human* rights. But we are not alone on this planet.

Carrying capacity *can* be defined in human terms: how many people, living in what ways, can the Earth support? But it should not be so exclusively defined. By the same token, to speak of 'biological resources' or 'capital' in the usual way is deeply anthropocentric. As I hope this book has made clear, to assume that the planet's entire biomass is at our sole disposal is ethically reprehensible.

David Willey is quite right that fewer people would mean an overall better quality of life for all: fewer houses (less urbanization), fewer cars (less road-building and congestion), fuller employment, higher incomes and 'a harder life for pathogens'.[31] He also includes less intensive agriculture and factory farming, and more countryside. This is all quite true and important, but ethically speaking it rather stops short. *It would also mean a better life for the natural world –* a world that includes, but greatly exceeds, us.

# Postscript

In the course of this book, we have considered the problems with much the greater part of existing ethics – whether religious, secular, utilitarian or deontological – when it comes to recognizing and rising to the challenge of global ecocrisis. Those limitations centre on anthropocentrism as a perspective which locates virtually all value in humanity as distinct from nature. It includes related dynamics such as an objectifying attitude to non-human nature and the accompanying instrumentalist ethos which sanctions its undue exploitation, i.e. 'resourcism'; a rigid distinction between human and non-human life and the systematic privileging of the former, i.e. 'speciesism'; and the narrow and short-term character of so-called enlightened self-interest.

We then explored a much more promising kind of ethics, namely ecocentric. That was defined, in its fullest sense, as one which (1) locates value in the more-than-human world – the Earth, or nature as such, including but vastly exceeding humanity; (2) is holistic, thus extending to both species and places; and (3) is impartial in relation to conflicts between human and non-human nature. Various such ethics were examined, especially of the dark or deep green kind.

It was further suggested that an ecocentric ethics is ideally pluralist and pragmatic, post-secular and part of a programme of green
citizenship based on a virtue ethics that also draws on civic republicanism and ecofeminism.

I have argued that such an ethics is not only desirable but
urgently needed. It remains an open question, of course, the extent
to which it is feasible. That will ultimately depend on the collective human answer to a question posed by the authors of a book on
Easter Island, whose now extinct inhabitants

> carried out for us the experiment of permitting unrestricted popula-
> tion growth, profligate use of resources, destruction of the environ-
> ment and boundless confidence in their religion to take care of the
> future. The result was an ecological disaster leading to a population
> crash. . . . Do we have to repeat the experiment on [a] grand scale?[1]

And as I have been at pains to point out, the effects of an ecological
disaster, even if it is human-caused, are by no means restricted to
humans.

In this book we have considered many different kinds and aspects
of ecological ethics. Some have survived critical examination better
than others. Even concerning those, however – and let us take 'ecological spirituality' as an example – it could be asked, should we
adopt it because it is true or because it would be good for the Earth?
But the very way this question is posed, in the distinction between
'true' and 'good' which it assumes as fundamental, carries within it
a non-ecological sensibility; so it cannot be answered in its own
terms without betraying the ecocentrism it questions. As David
Abram reminds us,

> Ecologically speaking, it is not primarily our verbal statements that are
> 'true' or 'false,' but rather the kind of relations that we sustain with the
> rest of nature. A human community that lives in a mutually beneficial
> relation with the surrounding earth is a community, we might say, that
> lives in truth. . . . [Whereas] A civilization that relentlessly destroys the
> living land it inhabits is not well acquainted with *truth*, regardless of
> how many supposed facts it has amassed regarding the calculable prop-
> erties of its world. (1996: 264)

What such a question, and the attitude that informs it, forgets is that we cannot stand outside the Earth and judge its value or truth from elsewhere, or nowhere. Ultimately, nature is what enables us to do anything, including assess truth; so barring a collective death-wish, we can only consider it not only a good but for us and all other Earthlings, the ultimate good.

For the same reason – which is to say, an inclusive ecology – to 'know' or 'assess' or 'consider' is not possible without participating in a relationship with what is being known, assessed or considered. These do not *precede* acting: they are already actions, and an ethical dimension is therefore present from the start.

Aldo Leopold once observed that 'One of the penalties of an ecological education is one lives alone in a world of wounds' (1993: 165). It is indeed often painful, but to recognize that world and those wounds is the first step to healing.

# Notes

## Chapter 1    Introduction

1 E.g., Kohak 2000; Des Jardins 2001; Wenz 2001; Benson 2000.
2 The term 'ethical extensionism' was first used, I believe, by Singer 1981.
3 There is a precedent for my choice: Kohak 2000.
4 See Cooper 1992.
5 See Smith 1988: 160.

## Chapter 2    The Earth in Crisis

1 For excellent overviews, see Ponting 1991, 2000.
2 E.g., North 1995; Easterbrook 1995; Lomberg 2001. For scientific critiques of the latter, see reports by the Danish Committee on Scientific Dishonesty (7.1.03) and the Danish Ecological Council (28.6.03), and in the pages of those bastions of fringe radical environmentalism, *Nature* (8.11.01) and *Scientific American* (1.02).
3 See the annual UNEP Global Environmental Reports, or those of the Worldwatch Institute and World Resource Institute, e.g. WRI 2002. The most recent one at the time of writing is that of 2003 for 2003–4. See also IGBP 2001. See also McNeill 2001, although his neglect of

modern capitalism as the principal engine of environmental change is extraordinary; see the review by Donald Worster, 'On the planet of the apes', *Times Literary Supplement* (13.7.01), p. 12. See also Ponting 1991, 1997.

4 IPCC 2001.

5 See Speth 2004; Gelbspan 2004.

6 'Put us all on rations', *The Guardian* (26.8.04). For a good layperson's discussion, see Verlyn Klinkenborg, 'Be afraid. Be very afraid', *The New York Times Book Review* (30.5.04).

7 UNEP, 'Global Environment Outlook 3: Past, Present and Future Perspectives' (2002).

8 Lord (Robert) May (President of the Royal Society) and Janet Larsen (Earth Policy Institute), quoted in the *Guardian* (2.10.03 and 10.3.04 respectively). See also Leakey and Lewin 1996.

9 Figures from the International Union for the Conservation of Nature, and the *Guardian* (22.7.04).

10 Gardner-Outlaw and Engelman 1999: 26.

11 Richard Aronson, Dauphin Island Sea Lab (*Guardian* 19.2.04).

12 Smil 1993: 181.

13 E.g., Solomon et al. 2003; IUCN/UNEP 2003.

14 *Environmental Health Perspectives* 112: 5 (April 2004).

15 Thomas 2004.

16 Speaking at the February 2004 meeting of the AAAS (*Guardian*, 14.2.04).

17 Jones 1993.

18 The original idea is usually attributed to Paul and Anne Erhlich, but I have been unable to find the exact first reference. But for a good discussion see Sylvan and Bennett 1994: 36–53. I am grateful to Harry Cripps for his suggestions in this section.

19 From p. 11 of a paper written by David Willey for the Optimum Population Trust entitled 'Some Hopes and Thoughts for the Future' (September 2000).

20 UN Population Division 2002.

21 The question of measuring affluence is vexed. The most prevalent measures (e.g., Gross Domestic Product and Gross National Product) are not very realistic ones.

22 Forman 1997.

23 See the analysis in Ekins 1992.

24  This led Paul Feyerabend (1978: 106–7) to argue that 'Science is one ideology among many and should be separated from the state just as religion is now separated from the state.'

25  See, e.g., Feyerabend 1978, 1987; Midgley 1992, 2001.

26  See Bauer 1994.

27  On pain of circularity.

28  See Bulger et al. 1995; Jasanoff 1990; Horton 2004.

29  See Stenmark 2001.

30  See Bulger et al. 1995; Jasanoff 1990; Horton 2004.

31  This is what Paul Feyerabend (1987) called 'democratic relativism'. See also Midgley's excellent work (1992, 2001). The same point was made much earlier, of course, by (e.g.) William James and Max Weber.

32  Latour continues: 'Reality is not defined by matters of fact. Matters of fact are only very partial and very polemical, very political renderings of matters of concern. It is this second empiricism, this return to a realist attitude, that I'd like to offer as the next task for the critically minded' (2004: 18).

## Chapter 3  Ethics

1  For a good introduction, see Blackburn 2001.

2  See Smith 1998 and Curry 2000.

3  I am running together the metaphysical and epistemological aspects of both realism and relativism, but in an introductory context the distinction seems to me unnecessarily confusing. For the same reason, I will stick with the commonly posited opposition between realism and relativism (rather than calling the latter, say, 'anti-realism').

4  See the excellent discussion in Smith 1997: ch. 5.

5  The best discussion of these issues is in Smith 1988, 1997; but see also Latour 1993: ch. 4; Feyerabend 1987: ch. 1.

6  From Hume 1740; Moore 1903.

7  Philosophers of science call the first point the 'theory-laden' nature of facts, and the second the 'underdetermination of theory by facts'.

8  With thanks to Nigel Cooper for this point.

9  Kohak 2000: 137.

10  I have borrowed this useful word, and idea, from the philosopher Henry Corbin, who used it to denote the non-physical but not therefore (like 'imaginary') non-real.

11 With thanks to Michael Novack for pointing this out.
12 By those who have wanted to understand it that way. Cf. Kohak 2000: 62–3.
13 See also Psalms 96: 11–13, 148: 9–10, 13.
14 See Haught 1996.
15 See Shklar 1984. (Christ specified that blasphemy against the Holy Ghost was unforgivable: Matthew 12: 31.)
16 See Henry 2002.
17 Among its exemplars are Richard Dawkins, Peter Atkins and Lewis Wolpert. By way of contrast, see the work of Mary Midgley, Barbara Herrnstein Smith and, of course – presciently – Paul Feyerabend.
18 The late Marcello Truzzi was a good and, unfortunately, rare example of a modern sceptic.
19 See Ehrenfeld 1981.
20 Although the contract was among subjects about the state, not directly with the state (a point which I owe to an anonymous reviewer).
21 I have borrowed this basic analysis from Ekins 1992; see also Toulmin's excellent 1990; Scott 1998; and Bauman 1992.

## Chapter 4    Three Schools of Ethics

1 Fox 1984; Frasz 1993; Wensveem 2000; Swanton 2004.
2 I take some comfort from the extent of disagreement about Kant among professional philosophers themselves.
3 I have been helped here by Scruton's discussion in his 2001.
4 *On the Basis of Morality*, p. 83; quoted in Janaway 2002: 90.
5 See Janaway 2002: 92.
6 See the criticisms in Gray 1993.
7 See Skinner 1998.
8 That is, preferences can be criticized, but not on preference-utilitarian grounds.
9 With thanks to Michael Novack for help with this point.
10 See Scott 1998.

## Chapter 5    Value

1 E.g., Callicott 1985.
2 Cf. Smith 1988, 1997; in relation to ecocentrism and intrinsic value, see Curry 2003.

3  E.g., respectively, Rolston 1997 and Callicott 1985; again, see Curry 2003.

4  Jordanova is actually taking Keith Thomas, in his *Man and the Natural World* (1983), to task for being insufficiently anthropocentric. (Emphasis in the original.)

5  See also Fox 1995: 20–2 for a good discussion.

6  Hayward 1994, 1997.

7  Respectively: as first suggested by Routley and Routley 1979; Ryder 1973; Eckersley 1998; see also Hayward 1998.

8  See Bahro 1994.

9  A term I have borrowed from David Orton.

10  It is by no means impossible, nor unknown, to prefer at least some non-human animals to other humans.

11  There may be a case for (or at least a parallel with) 'ecologism'. The problem is the latter has at least three current and highly conflicting meanings: ecological philosophy (Dobson), extremist ecological ideology (Bramwell), and eco-scientism (Naess).

12  See Eckersley 1992.

13  See Snyder 1990.

14  This is consistent theme in the work of Murray Bookchin among other social ecologists.

15  See Hargrove 1989.

16  See Abram's excellent 1996.

17  See Evernden 1985.

## Chapter 6    Light Green or Shallow (Anthropocentric) Ethics

1  'Light green' comes from Sylvan and Bennett 1994, 'shallow' from Naess's influential 1973.

2  With thanks to Michael Novack for the points in this paragraph.

3  I owe the formulation of this point directly to an anonymous reviewer of the MS.

4  The term 'magmachine' is Lewis Mumford's.

5  Such as Botkin 1992; Budiansky 1995; Easterbrook 1995.

6  E.g., Pearce et al. 1989.

7  The reference is, of course, to Rudyard Kipling's notorious justification of imperialism as 'the white man's burden'.

8  For an excellent analysis of the scale of scientistic fantasy, see Midgley 1992.

9  E.g., Bookchin 1990.
10 Cf. the excellent critique by Eckersley 1989.
11 See also Livingstone 1981; Ehrenfeld 1981.
12 Terry Hamblin, quoted in the *Guardian* (8.8.98), G2 section, p. 20.
13 The seminal text here is Polanyi 1957.
14 Cf. Ostrom 1990.
15 With thanks to Michael Novack and Nigel Cooper for clarifying this
   point.

## Chapter 7   Mid-Green or Intermediate Ethics

1  Cf. Curry 2000.
2  See Sylvan and Bennett 1994: 85.
3  See Gellatley 1996.
4  Ibid. See also, e.g., Spencer 1993.
5  *Viva!/Life* (Spring 2004): 5; *The Guardian* (25.8.04): 17. See Pimentel
   and Pimentel 1996; Lappe 1992.
6  See Coetzee 1999.
7  'Who' is appropriate for any subject or agent, just as 'that' or 'what' are
   appropriate for any object. It is therefore incorrect to limit the former
   term to human beings; we are human because we are (a kind of)
   subject, not subjects because we are human beings.
8  The term was first coined by Ryder 1973.

## Chapter 8   Dark Green or Deep (Ecocentric) Ethics

1  Sylvan and Bennett 1994: 90.
2  Cf. Pimentel et al. 2000.
3  I came into possession of a copy too late to draw upon it for this book,
   but Bender 2004 is clearly an important new analysis of ecocentrism.
4  Such as is being developed, in different ways, by people like Susan
   Bratton, Jane Lubchenko and Carl Safina (with thanks to Jack Stillwell
   for this point).
5  Sylvan and Bennett assign the Land Ethic to Intermediate
   Environmental Ethics, a decision with which I do not agree.
   (Leopold's moral extensionism is not, in itself, sufficient grounds.)
6  He was preceded by Bateson 1972, 1979.
7  See Curry 2000.

8 Those are the three Buddhist 'sins', which seem to me to be ecologically more relevant than the Christian ones.

9 See Smith 1988, 1997 and Latour 1993.

10 As for developing a genetically modified cow resistant to BSE –
something which was reported in 2004 – that is simply and in every
sense sad.

11 See Curry 2003; Viveiros de Castro 2002.

12 Lovelock 1979, 1988.

13 See the bibliography in Bunyard 1996.

14 E.g., Margulis, in Bunyard 1996: 54.

15 See Abram 1996. The objection also ignores the considerable subsequent work modelling Gaia (e.g., 'Daisyworld').

16 See Rawles 1996.

17 With thanks to Clay Ramsay for points I have incorporated here.

18 See Quammen 1998, 1999.

19 As Machiavelli argued.

20 Margulis, in Bunyard 1996: 64; Lovelock 1991.

21 See also David Rothenberg, in Naess 1989.

22 Taken from Naess 1989: 29. These differ slightly (but not substantively) from the way they are stated in Devall and Sessions 1985.

23 Naess 1989: 28; Naess and Sessions 1984.

24 For a very different (and preferable) definition of depth ecology, see
Abram 2005.

25 See Chase 1991 for a good summary.

26 See Sylvan and Bennett 1994: 99–102.

27 See also Fox 1995: 223–4.

28 See Sylvan and Bennett 1994: 102–4, 107–10; also Katz 2000.

29 In Mahayana Buddhism, a Bodhisattva is one who is ready to transcend
the world of suffering (*samsara*) for *nirvana* but chooses instead to stay,
or return, in order to help others.

30 See Bateson 1972, 1979; Abram 1996. (Not idealism in the sense of
having ideals, but in the philosophical sense of according the spiritual
primacy over the material world.)

31 See Barry 1999; Curry 2000.

32 Plumwood 1995.

33 See Abram 1996: 66–7.

34 Li 1998: 300.

35 Salleh adds that 'There is surely a large portion of illusion and self-

indulgence in the North's comfortable middle-class pursuit of the cosmic "transpersonal Self" ' (1993: 229).

36  Cf. Abram 1996.

37  Perhaps apocryphal, but to the point nonetheless; I have also seen this remark attributed to T. S. Eliot.

38  With respect to David Bennett, whose role as Sylvan's co-author I am sure was crucial, I shall treat DGT as primarily the work of Sylvan. It is certainly of a piece with his earlier writing.

39  Cf. McLaughlin 1993: 214.

40  Such as those of Guhu 1989.

41  I'm afraid I cannot now locate the reference for this remark, and I would be grateful if any reader can supply it.

42  Email <greenweb@ca.inter.net>. I would like to thank David Orton for his helpful comments on this section.

43  <http://home.ca.inter.net/~greenweb/index.htm>. Extant at the time of writing.

44  At the time of writing, the members of the Left Bio list are considering revising and extending the Primer. It is unlikely, however, that a new version will depart substantively from the one discussed here.

45  Cf. Kohak 2000: 64.

46  For one well-informed answer in the negative, see Rees 2000.

47  McLaughlin 1993.

48  I am grateful to Penny Novack for the points in this paragraph.

49  Michael Novack, private communication.

50  David Orton, 'A Deep Ecology Talk' (4 July 2003).

51  See, e.g., McLaughlin 1993.

52  Imhoff et al. 2004; but cf. Vitousek et al. 1986 and Daily 1995, respectively.

53  Galadriel's words to Frodo in J. R. R. Tolkien's *The Lord of the Rings*. (For a qualified ecocentric reading of the latter, see Curry 2004.)

54  As Rudolf Bahro always insisted, to the disquiet of the socialist left.

55  Email <mosquin@ecospherics.net>. See also <http://www.ecospherics.net>.

56  Sadly, Stan Rowe died on 6 April 2004.

57  Earth Charter USA (2000). See the special issue of *Worldviews* 8: 1 (2004).

58  As with most other such statements discussed here, please see the

original document, which is freely available – in this case, at <www. earthcharter.org> – for the full text.

59 For a strong case, see Salleh 2000. I would like to thank Ariel Salleh for her patient and invaluable help with this section.

60 Cf. Plumwood 1993: 60.

61 See Merchant 1980; Keller 1985; Harding 1986.

62 Which makes Warren's (2000) dalliance with scientism all the more bizarre.

63 See Salleh 1984.

64 See Salleh 1997; Warren 1994; Plumwood 1993.

65 Gilligan 1982; Noddings 1984; Ruddick 1989.

66 For supportive philosophical argument (excepting his occasional lapses into scientism), see Williams 1993. On the wrecks, see Scott 1998.

## Chapter 9   Deep Green Ethics as Post-Secular

1 Note the typically light touch in his subtitle.

2 See Weber 1991: 143, 153; Midgley 1992, 2001; Feyerabend 1978.

3 Or what Max Weber (1991: 282) called 'concrete magic'. Cf. Bateson 1972, 1979; Abram 1996.

4 I am grateful, here as elsewhere, to Nigel Cooper and Michael Winship for obliging me to be more fair-minded, at least, than I sometimes tend to be!

5 See, for example, the fundamental distinction between religion and enchantment made by Max Weber 1991: 129–56.

6 See Curry 1999.

7 Abram's (1996) excellent term.

8 Which the Dalai Lama and Vaclav Havel, among others, have advocated.

9 Anderson 1996.

10 See Deloria 2000 for an excellent review of Krech 1999.

11 Personal communication (28.11.03).

12 See, e.g., Salleh 1997; Plumwood 2002. See also Curry 2000; Clifford and King 1996.

13 See Bird-David 1999; Viveiros de Castro 1998; Harvey 2005.

## Chapter 10   Moral Pluralism and Pragmatism

1 See James 1977; Weber's seminal essay 'On Science as a Vocation' in his 1991; Berlin 1969 and his superb essay 'The Originality of Machiavelli' in his 1998.
2 See also Kontos 1994.
3 Abram 1996; Weston 1994.
4 On epistemological pluralism, see Feyerabend 1987 and Smith 1997; on axiological (value) pluralism see Smith's exemplary 1988; on moral pluralism, see Berlin 1969; on pluralism in a political context, and in relation to ecocentrism, see Stone 1987, 1995; Brennan 1995, 1995b; Midgley 1997; Curry 2003.
5 Brennan 1995.
6 See Stone 1995; Brennan 1995b; also Laclau and Mouffe 1985.
7 She adds: 'The idea that reductive simplicity here is particularly rational or "scientific" is mere confusion' (1997: 100).
8 This is also something that Machiavelli and Weber recognized.
9 See Swanton 2004.
10 I am thinking of the work of William James and John Dewey (more than Pierce).
11 See Plumwood 2002: 124–6.

## Chapter 11   Green Citizenship

1 Clay Ramsay, personal communication.
2 See Smith 1988: 132.
3 Cf. Norton 1991.
4 See Jones 1993 for an excellent discussion.
5 Cf. Barry 1999: 233.
6 See Sandel 1996; Pettit 1997; Oldfield 1990; and in an ecological context, Curry 2000.
7 See Tam 1998, for a promising (although non-ecocentric) version.
8 See especially Salleh 1997.
9 See Curry 2000. 'Life' here is intended to include the abiotic whose matrix it shares, as discussed above.
10 See Raphals 1992.
11 Tucker and Berthrong 1998; Chan 1963; Montaigne 1991.
12 With thanks to Michael Novack for reminding me of this wonderful passage.

Chapter 12    A Case-Study: Human Overpopulation

1  Quoted in the Optimum Population Trust (OPT) Newsletter (January 1998): 6.
2  Cf. the *British Medical Journal* 319 (9.10.99): 931–4, 977–97.
3  See Ehrenfeld 1981.
4  See too the point about human appropriation of global photosynthetic energy, made in the section on Left Bio.
5  With thanks to Harry Cripps for clarifying this point.
6  WWF 2002.
7  Ted Mosquin, personal communication.
8  In addition to the authors directly cited or quoted, much good thinking respecting all three concepts is carried out by members of the UK-based Optimum Population Trust (OPT).
9  Alec Ponton, *The Pherologist* 4: 3 (August 2001): 2.
10  See Youngquist 1999.
11  Also see Rees 1996.
12  Including, as Gaia Theory and the Earth Manifesto do, the inorganic elements that are essential to life.
13  Willey 2000; Smail 1997; Ferguson 1999 (and writings in general for the OPT). See the entire issue that includes Smail's paper, that is, pp. 181–354, for an excellent discussion.
14  Cf. Stanton 2004.
15  Walter Schwarz, 'Crowd control', *Guardian* (1.9.04).
16  This analysis is indebted to that of Irvine 2000.
17  Willey 1997.
18  Virginia Abernethy, *The Pherologist* 2: 3 (1999): 7 (with references).
19  Another analogy might be: responding to a growing debt by repeatedly increasing the overdraft limit – as if this could be kept up indefinitely.
20  Once again I would appreciate learning the reference for this quotation (which I have no reason to doubt).
21  John Guillebaud, quoted in letter by Doeke Oostra of EPOC (6.2.01).
22  To quote Paul Watson (statement issued in November 2003): 'I don't believe it is anti-immigrant to be in favor of lower immigration levels for the same reason I don't think it is anti-baby to be in favor of less babies being born.'
23  With thanks to Mike Novack for this point.
24  On this subject, see Kates 2004.

25 See Sandel 1996; Pettit 1997; Oldfield 1990; and in an ecological context, Curry 2000.

26 With thanks to Michael Novack for discussions concerning the last point.

27 Some non-academic books on this subject are: Casey 1998; Carroll 2000; Cain 2001.

28 See also the excellent paper by Kates 2004.

29 As called for by Smail 1997.

30 See Jensen and Draffan 2003.

31 Quoted in EPOC press release (14.2.99).

## Postscript

1 Paul Bahn and John Flenley, *Easter Island, Earth Island*; quoted by Ronald Wright in the *TLS*, 19.11.04. (I regret that I did not have time to obtain a copy before finishing the MS of this book.) See the excellent recent book by Diamond (2005).

# References

Abernethy, Virginia (1993) *Population Politics: The Choices that Shape Our Future* (New York: Plenum).

Abram, David (1996) *The Spell of the Sensuous: Perception and Language in a More-Than-Human World* (New York: Random House).

—— (1996b) 'The Mechanical and the Organic: Epistemological Consequences of the Gaia Hypothesis', in Bunyard (ed.).

—— (2005) 'Depth Ecology', in Taylor (ed.).

Adams, W. M. (2003) *Future Nature: A Vision for Conservation*, rev. edn. (London: Earthscan).

Alexander, F. M. (2000) *Aphorisms*, ed. Jean M. O. Fischer (London: Mouritz).

Anderson, E. N. (1996) *Ecologies of the Heart: Emotion, Belief, and the Environment* (Oxford: Oxford University Press).

Attfield, Robin (1983) *The Ethics of Environmental Concern* (Oxford: Blackwell).

Bahro, Rudolf (1986) *Building the Green Movement* (London: GMP).

—— (1994) *Avoiding Social and Ecological Disaster: The Politics of World Transformation*, rev. edn. (Bath: Gateway Books).

Barry, John (1999) *Rethinking Green Politics* (London: Sage).

Bateson, Gregory (1972) *Steps to an Ecology of Mind* (New York: Ballantine).

—— (1979) *Mind and Nature: A Necessary Unity* (New York: Dutton).

Bauer, Henry (1994) *Scientific Literacy and the Myth of the Scientific Method* (Urbana, IL: University of Illinois Press).

Bauman, Zygmunt (1992) *Intimations of Postmodernity* (London: Routledge).

Bender, Frederic L. (2004) *The Culture of Extinction: Toward a Philosophy of Deep Ecology* (Amherst: Humanity Books).

Benson, Jon (2000) *Environmental Ethics: An Introduction with Readings* (London: Routledge).

Bentham, Jeremy (1907) *The Principles of Morals and Legislation* (Oxford: Oxford University Press).

Berlin, Isaiah (1969) *Four Essays on Liberty* (Oxford: Oxford University Press).

—— (1998) *The Proper Study of Mankind: An Anthology of Essays*, ed. Henry Hardy and Roger Hausheer (London: Pimlico).

Birch, Thomas H. (2001) 'Moral Considerability and Universal Consideration', *Environmental Ethics* 23 (2): 313–32.

Bird-David, Nurit (1999) ' "Animism" Revisited: Personhood, Environment, and Relational Epistemology', *Current Anthropology* 40: S67–S91; reprinted in Graham Harvey (ed.), *Readings in Indigenous Religions* (London: Continuum, 2002): 73–105.

Blackburn, Simon (2001) *Being Good: A Short Introduction to Ethics* (Oxford: Oxford University Press).

—— (ed.) (1994) *The Oxford Dictionary of Philosophy* (Oxford: Oxford University Press).

Bookchin, Murray (1990) *The Philosophy of Social Ecology* (Montreal: Black Rose Books).

—— (1995) *Re-Enchanting Humanity: A Defense of the Human Spirit Against Antihumanism, Misanthropy, Mysticism and Primitivism* (London: Cassell).

Botkin, Daniel B. (1992) *Discordant Harmonies: New Ecology for the Twenty-First Century* (Oxford: Oxford University Press).

Bramwell, Anna (1989) *Ecology in the 20th Century* (New Haven: Yale University Press).

Brennan, Andrew (ed.) (1995) *The Ethics of the Environment* (Aldershot: Dartmouth).

—— (1995b) 'Ecological Theory and Value in Nature', in Elliott (ed.).

—— (1995c) 'Moral Pluralism and the Environment', in Brennan (ed.).

Brennan, Andrew (ed.) (1998) *Thinking About Nature: An Investigation of Nature, Value and Ecology* (London: Routledge).

Brennan, Teresa (2000) *Exhausting Modernity: Grounds for a New Economy* (London: Routledge).

Briggs, Robert (2001) 'Wild Thoughts: A Deconstructive Environmental Ethics?', *Environmental Ethics* 23 (2): 115–34.

Brown, Lester (2000) 'Challenges of the New Century', *State of the World 2000* (New York: Norton).

Budiansky, Stephen (1995) *Nature's Keepers: The New Science of Nature Management* (London: Weidenfeld and Nicholson).

Bulger, Ruth Ellen, Bobby, Elizabeth Meyer and Fineberg, Harvey (eds) (1995) *Society's Choices* (Washington, DC: National Academy of Sciences).

Bunyard, Peter (ed.) (1996) *Gaia in Action: Science of the Living Earth* (Edinburgh: Floris Books).

Cain, Madelyn (2001) *The Childless Revolution: What it Means to be Childless Today* (New York: Perseus Publications).

Caldwell, John (2002) 'The Contemporary Population Challenge', *Expert Group Meeting on Completing the Fertility Transition* (New York: UNPD Department of Economic and Social Affairs).

Callicott, J. Baird (1985) 'Intrinsic Value, Quantum Theory, and Environmental Ethics', *Environmental Ethics* 7: 357–75.

—— (1989) *In Defence of the Land Ethic* (Albany, NY: State University of New York Press).

—— (ed.) (1987) *A Companion to the Sand County Almanac* (Madison: University of Wisconsin Press).

Capra, Fritjof (1997) *The Web of Life: A New Synthesis of Mind and Matter* (London: Flamingo).

Carroll, Laura (2000) *Families of Two: Interviews with Happily Married Couples without Children by Choice* (Philadelphia: Xlibris).

Casey, Terri (1998) *Pride and Joy: The Lives and Passions of Women without Children* (Hillsboro, OR: Beyond Words Publications).

Chan, Wing-Tsit (1963) *A Source Book in Chinese Philosophy* (Princeton: Princeton University Press).

Chappell, T. D. J. (ed.) (1997) *The Philosophy of the Environment* (Edinburgh: Edinburgh University Press).

Chase, Steve (ed.) (1991) *Defending the Earth: A Dialogue Between Murray Bookchin and Dave Foreman* (Boston: South End Press).

Cheetham, Tom (1993) 'The Forms of Life: Complexity, History, and Actuality', *Environmental Ethics* 15 (4): 293–311.

Clifford, Sue and King, Angela (1993) *Local Distinctiveness: Place, Particularity and Identity* (London: Common Ground).

Coetzee, J. M. (1999) *The Lives of Animals*, ed. Amy Gutman (Princeton: Princeton University Press).

Coleman, Jon (2004) *Vicious: Wolves and Men in America* (New Haven: Yale University Press).

Cooper, David E. (1992) 'The Idea of Environment', in Cooper and Palmer (eds).

Cooper, David E. and Palmer, Joy A. (eds) (1992) *The Environment in Question* (London: Routledge).

Curry, Patrick (1999) 'Magic vs. Enchantment', *Journal of Contemporary Religion* 14 (3): 401–12.

—— (2000) 'Redefining Community: Towards an Ecological Republicanism', *Biodiversity and Conservation* 9 (8): 1059–71.

—— (2003) 'Rethinking Nature: Towards an Ecopluralism', *Environmental Values* 12 (3): 337–60.

—— (2004) *Defending Middle-Earth: Tolkien, Myth and Modernity*, 2nd edn. (Boston: Houghton Mifflin).

Daly, Herman E. and Cobb, John B. (1990) *For the Common Good* (London: Green Print).

Daily, G. (1995) *People and the Planet* 4 (4): 18–19.

Deloria, Vine, Jr. (2000) 'The Speculations of Krech', *Worldviews* 4 (3): 283–93.

Des Jardins, Joseph R. (2001) *Environmental Ethics: An Introduction to Environmental Philosophy*, 3rd edn. (Belmont, CA: Wadsworth).

Devall, Bill and Sessions, George (1985) *Deep Ecology: Living as if Nature Mattered* (Salt Lake City: Peregrine Smith Books).

Diamond, Jared (2005) *Collapse: How Societies Choose to Fail or Succeed* (London: Allen Lane).

Dower, Nigel (2004) 'The Earth Charter and Global Ethics', *Worldviews* 8 (1): 15–28.

Drengson, Alan and Inoue, Yuichi (eds) (1995) *The Deep Ecology Movement: An Introductory Anthology* (Berkeley: North Atlantic Books).

Duguid, James P. (2004) *Population, Resources, and the Quality of Life*, 2nd edn., ed. Jack Parsons (Llantrisant: Population Policy Press).

Earth Charter USA (2000) *Exploring the Earth Charter: Resources for*

*Community Study* (Washington, DC: Earth Charter USA); available from <www.earth-charterusa.org/resources>.

Easterbrook, Gregg (1995) *A Moment on the Earth* (New York: Penguin Books).

Eckersley, Robyn (1989) 'Divining Evolution: The Ecological Ethics of Murray Bookchin', *Environmental Ethics* 11: 99–116.

—— (1992) *Environmentalism and Political Theory: Toward an Ecocentric Approach* (Albany: State University of New York Press).

—— (1998) 'Beyond Human Racism', *Environmental Values* 7: 165–82.

Erlich, Anne and Erlich, Paul (1990) *The Population Explosion* (New York: Simon & Schuster).

Ehrenfeld, David (1976) 'The Conservation of Non-Resources', *American Scientist* 64: 648–56.

—— (1981) *The Arrogance of Humanism*, 2nd edn. (Oxford: Oxford University Press).

Ekins, Paul (1992) *A New World Order: Grassroots Movements for Global Change* (London: Routledge).

Elliott, Robert (ed.) (1995) *Environmental Ethics* (Oxford: Oxford University Press).

Evernden, Neil (1985) *The Natural Alien: Humankind and Environment* (Toronto: University of Toronto Press).

—— (1992) *The Social Construction of Nature* (Baltimore: Johns Hopkins University Press).

Fagan, Brian (2004) 'Ice Age Ahead Will Sink Us if We Kill Current of Life', *THES* (7 May): 16–17.

Ferguson, A. R. B. (1999) 'The Logical Foundations of Ecological Footprints', *Environment, Development and Sustainability* 2: 149–56.

Ferry, Luc (1995) *The New Ecological Order*, trans. Carol Volk (Chicago: Chicago University Press).

Feyerabend, Paul (1978) *Science in a Free Society* (London: NLB).

—— (1987) *Farewell to Reason* (London: Verso).

—— (1995) *Killing Time* (Chicago: University of Chicago Press).

Forman, Paul (1997) 'Recent Science: Late-Modern and Post-Modern', in Söderqvist, Thomas (ed.), *The Historiography of Contemporary Science and Technology* (Amsterdam: Harwood Academic).

Fowles, John (1979) *The Tree* (St Albans: The Sumach Press).

Fox, Warwick (1984) 'Deep Ecology: A New Philosophy of Our Time?', *The Ecologist* 14 (7): 194–200.

—— (1986) 'Approaching Deep Ecology: A Response to Richard Sylvan's Critique of Deep Ecology', Hobart: University of Tasmania, Environmental Studies. Occasional paper 20.

—— (1995) *Toward a Transpersonal Ecology: Developing New Foundations for Environmentalism* (Foxhole: Resurgence).

—— (2000) 'Deep Ecology and Virtue Ethics', *Philosophy Now* (April/May): 21–3.

Frasz, Geoffrey B. (1993) 'Environmental Virtue Ethics: A New Direction for Environmental Ethics', *Environmental Ethics* 15: 259–74.

Gardner-Outlaw, Tom and Engelman, Robert (1999) *Forest Futures: Population, Consumption and Wood Resources* (Population Action International).

Gelbspan, Ross (2004) *Boiling Point: How Politicians, Big Oil and Coal, Journalists, and Activists are Fueling the Climate Crisis – and What We Can Do to Avert Disaster* (New York: Basic Books).

Gellatley, Juliet, with Tony Wardle (1996) *The Silent Ark* (London: HarperCollins).

Gilligan, Carol (1982) *In a Different Voice: Psychological Theory and Women's Development* (Cambridge, MA: Harvard University Press).

—— (1987) 'Moral Orientation and Moral Development', in E. Feder Kitlay and D. Meyos (eds), *Women and Moral Theory* (Totowa, NJ: Rowman and Littlefield).

—— (1994) 'Reply to my Critics', in Mary Jeanne Larabee (ed.), *An Ethic of Care: Feminist and Interdisciplinary Perspectives* (London: Routledge).

Gray, John (1993) *Post-Liberalism: Studies in Political Thought* (London: Routledge).

Grey, William (1993) 'Anthropocentrism and Deep Ecology', *Australasian Journal of Philosophy* 71 (4): 463–75.

—— (2000) 'A Critique of Deep Green Theory', in Katz et al. (eds).

Guhu, Ramachandra (1989) 'Radical American Environmentalism and Wilderness Preservation: A Third World Critique', *Environmental Ethics* 11: 71–83.

Hardin, Garrett (1968) 'The Tragedy of the Commons', *Science* 162: 1243–8; reprinted in Jon Benson, *Environmental Ethics: An Introduction with Readings* (London: Routledge, 2000).

Hardin, Garrett (1974) 'The Tragedy of the Commons', *Bioscience* 24 (October): 561–8.

—— (1992) *Living within Limits: Ecology, Economics and Population Taboos* (New York: Oxford University Press).

Harding, Sandra (1996) *The Science Question in Feminism* (Ithaca: Cornell University Press).

Hargrove, Eugene C. (1989) *Foundations of Environmental Ethics* (Denton, TX: Environmental Ethics Books).

Harvey, Graham (2005) *Animism* (London: Hurst & Co).

Haught, John F. (1996) 'Christianity and Ecology', in Roger S. Gottlieb (ed.), *This Sacred Earth: Religion, Nature, Environment* (New York: Routledge).

Hayward, Tim (1994) *Ecological Thought: An Introduction* (Cambridge: Polity).

—— (1998) *Political Theory and Ecological Values* (Cambridge: Polity).

Henry, John (2002) *The Scientific Revolution and the Origins of Modern Science*, 2nd edn (Basingstoke: Palgrave).

Hooker, C. A. (1992) 'Responsibility, Ethics and Nature', in Cooper and Palmer (eds).

Horton, Richard (2004) 'The Dawn of McScience'. Review of Sheldon Krimsky's *Science in the Private Interest*, *New York Review of Books* 51 (4) (14 March).

Hume, David (1740) *A Treatise on Human Nature* (Oxford).

IGBP (2001) *Global Change and the Earth System: A Planet under Pressure*, Science Series No. 4, ed. Will Steffen and Peter Tyson (Stockholm: IGBP).

Imhoff, Marc L., Bounoua, Lahouari, Ricketts, Taylor, Loucks, Colby, Harriss, Robert and Lawrence, William T. (2004) 'Global Patterns in Human Consumption of Net Primary Production', *Nature* 429 (6994): 870–3.

IPCC (2001) *Climate Change 2001: Synthesis Report* (Intergovernmental Panel on Climate Change).

Irvine, Sandy (2001) *The Deeply Green Book Guide* (Newcastle upon Tyne: Real World Publishing).

—— (2002) 'Missing Numbers: The Overpopulation Denial Syndrome' (unpublished MS) (available at <www.ecopaedia.info>).

IUCN/UNEP (2003) *2003 World Database on Protected Areas*; CD-ROM.

James, William (1977/1909) *A Pluralistic Universe* (Cambridge, MA: Harvard University Press).

Janaway, Christopher (2002) *Schopenhauer: A Very Short Introduction* (Oxford: Oxford University Press).

Jasanoff, Sheila (1990) *The Fifth Branch: Science Advisers as Policymakers* (Cambridge, MA: Harvard University Press).

Jensen, Derrick and Draffan, George (2003) *Strangely Like a War: The Global Assault on Forests* (White River Junction, VT: Chelsea Green Publishing Co).

Jones, Ken (1993) *Beyond Optimism: A Buddhist Political Ecology* (Oxford: Jon Carpenter Publishing).

Jordanova, Ludmilla (1987) 'The Interpretation of Nature: A Review Article', *Comparative Studies in Society and History* 27 (1): 195–200.

Kane, Sean (1994) *Wisdom of the Mythtellers* (Peterborough: Broadview Press).

Kates, Carol A. (2004) 'Reproductive Liberty and Overpopulation', *Environmental Values* 13 (1): 51–79.

Katz, Eric (2000) 'Against the Inevitability of Anthropocentrism', in Katz et al. (eds).

Katz, Eric, Light, Andrew and Rothenberg, David (eds.) (2000) *Beneath the Surface: Critical Essays in the Philosophy of Deep Ecology* (Cambridge, MA; MIT Press).

Keller, Evelyn Fox (1985) *Reflections on Gender and Science* (New Haven: Yale University Press).

King, Maurice and Elliott, Charles (1997) 'To the Point of Farce: A Martian View of the Hardinian Taboo – The Silence that Surrounds Population Control', *British Medical Journal* 315 (29 November): 1441–3.

Kohak, Erazim (2000) *The Green Halo: A Bird's-Eye View of Ecological Ethics* (Chicago & La Salle: Open Court).

Kontos, Alkis (1994) 'The World Disenchanted, and the Return of Gods and Demons', in Asher Horowitz and Terry Maley (eds), *The Barbarism of Reason: Max Weber and the Twilight of Reason* (Toronto: University of Toronto Press).

Krech, Shepherd (1999) *The Ecological Indian* (New York: W. W. Norton and Company).

Kundera, Milan (1984) *The Unbearable Lightness of Being* (London: Faber & Faber).

Laclau, Ernesto, *New Reflections on the Revolution of Our Time* (London: Verso).

Lappe, Frances Moore (1992) *Diet for a Small Planet* (New York: Ballantine).

Latour, Bruno (1993) *We Have Never Been Modern*, trans. Catherine Porter (Hemel Hempstead: Harvester Wheatsheaf).

—— (2004) 'Why Has Critique Run Out of Steam?', *Harper's Magazine* (April): 15–22; repr. from *Critical Inquiry* (Winter 2004).

Leakey, Richard and Lewin, Roger (1996) *The Sixth Extinction: Biodiversity and its Survival* (London: Weidenfeld & Nicolson).

Leopold, Aldo (1948) *A Sand County Almanac with Essays on Conservation from Round River* (New York: Oxford University Press); subsequent edns include Ballantine Books, 1970, 1990.

—— (1991) *The River of the Mother of God and Other Essays*, ed. Flader, Susan and Callicott, J. Baird (Madison: University of Wisconsin Press).

—— (1993) *Round River* (New York: Oxford University Press).

Li, Huey-li (1998) 'Some Thoughts on Confucianism and Ecofeminism', in Mary Evelyn Tucker and John Berthrong (eds), *Confucianism and Ecology* (Cambridge, MA: Harvard University Press).

Livingstone, John (1981) *The Fallacy of Wildlife Conservation* (Toronto: McClelland and Stewart).

Lohmann, Larry (2003) 'Re-Imagining the Population Debate', Corner House Briefing No. 28. Available at <www.thecornerhouse.org.uk/briefing/28reimag.html> (accessed 16.3.03).

Lomberg, Bjorn (2001) *The Skeptical Environmentalist: Measuring the Real State of the World* (Cambridge: Cambridge University Press).

Lovelock, James (1979) *Gaia: A New Look at Life on Earth* (Oxford: Oxford University Press).

—— (1988) *The Ages of Gaia: A Biography of our Living Earth* (New York: Norton).

—— (1991) *Healing Gaia: Practical Medicine for the Planet* (New York: Harmony).

Lutton, Wayne (2001) 'Garrett Hardin: An Introduction and Appreciation', *The Social Contract* 12 (1) (Fall); accessible at <http://www.thesocialcontract.com>.

Lynn, William S. (2004) 'Situating the Earth Charter: An Introduction', *Worldviews* 8 (1): 1–14.

Machiavelli, Niccolò (1981) *The Prince*, trans. George Bull (London: Penguin).

Mackey, Brendan G. (2004) 'The Earth Charter and Ecological Integrity – Some Policy Implications', *Worldviews* 8 (1): 76–92.

Maturana, Humberto and Varela, Francisco (1987) *The Tree of Knowledge: The Biological Roots of Human Understanding* (Boston: New Science Library).

McKibben, Bill (1990) *The End of Nature* (London: Penguin).

McLaughlin, Andrew (1993) 'Marxism and the Mastery of Nature: An Ecological Critique', in Roger S. Gottleib and Richard Schmitt (eds), *Radical Philosophy: Tradition, Counter-Tradition, Politics* (Philadelphia: Temple University Press).

—— (1993b) *Regarding Nature: Industrialism and Deep Ecology* (Albany: State University of New York Press).

McNeill, J. R. (2001) *Something New Under the Sun: An Environmental History of the Twentieth-Century World* (London: Allen Lane).

Meadows, Donella, Randers, Jorgen and Meadows, Dennis (2004) *Limits to Growth*, rev. edn. (White River Junction, VT: Chelsea Green).

Merchant, Carolyn (1980) *The Death of Nature: Women, Ecology and the Scientific Revolution* (San Francisco: Harper & Row).

—— (1995) *Earthcare: Women and the Environment* (New York: Routledge).

Midgley, Mary (1992) *Science as Salvation: A Modern Myth and its Meaning* (London: Routledge).

—— (1997) 'Sustainability and Moral Pluralism', in Chappell (ed.).

—— (2001) *Science and Poetry* (London: Routledge).

Milton, Kay (2002) *Loving Nature: Towards an Ecology of Emotion* (London: Routledge).

Montaigne, Michel de (1991) *The Complete Essays*, trans. M. A. Screech (London: Penguin Books).

Moore, G. E. (1903) *Principia Ethica* (Cambridge University Press).

Mosquin, Ted and Rowe, Stan (2004) 'A Manifesto for Earth', *Biodiversity* 5 (1): 3-9. Available at <www.ecospherics.net>.

Myers, Norman (1993) 'The Big Squeeze', *Earthwatch* (Nov/Dec): 25–30.

—— (1998) 'Population: Some Overlooked Issues', *The Environmentalist* 18: 135–8.

Naess, Arne (1973) 'The Shallow and the Deep, Long-Range Ecology Movements', *Inquiry* 16: 95–100.

—— (1987) 'Self-Realization: An Ecological Approach to Being in the World', *The Trumpeter* 4: 35–42; repr. in Drengson and Inoue (eds) 1995.

—— (1989) *Ecology, Community and Lifestyle*, ed. David Rothenberg (Cambridge: Cambridge University Press).

—— (1999) 'Paul Feyerabend: A Green Hero?' in Witoszek and Brennan (eds).

Naess, Arne and Sessions, George (1984) 'Basic Principles of Deep Ecology', *Ecophilosophy* 6: 3–7.

—— (1985) 'Platform Principles of the Deep Ecology Movement', in Bill

Devall and George Sessions, *Deep Ecology: Living as if Nature Mattered* (Salt Lake City: Peregrine Smith Books).

Nagel, Thomas (1986) *The View from Nowhere* (Oxford: Oxford University Press).

Noddings, Nel (1984) *Caring: A Feminine Approach to Ethics and Moral Education* (Berkeley: University of California Press).

North, Richard D. (1995) *Life on a Modern Planet: A Manifesto for Progress* (Manchester: University of Manchester Press).

Norton, Bryan (1991) *Toward Unity Among Environmentalists* (New York: Oxford University Press).

Oelschlaeger, Max (ed.) (1995) *Postmodern Environmental Ethics* (Albany: State University of New York Press).

Oldfield, Adrian (1990) *Citizenship and Community: Civic Republicanism and the Modern World* (London: Routledge).

Orr, David W. (2003) 'Walking North on a Southbound Train', *Rachel's Environment & Health News* 766 (3 April). Available at <http://www.rachel.org>.

Orton, David *Green Web Publications: Bulletins (Part I), Bulletins (Part II), and Book Reviews and Other Articles.* Available at <http://home.ca.inter.net/~greenweb/index.htm>.

Ostrom, Elinor (1990) *Governing the Commons: The Evolution of Institutions for Collective Action* (Cambridge: Cambridge University Press).

Parsons, Jack (1971) *Population versus Liberty* (London: Pemberton Publishing Co).

—— (1977) *Population Fallacies* (London: Elek Books Ltd).

Passmore, John (1974) *Man's Responsibility for Nature*, 2nd edn. (London: Duckworth).

Pearce, David, Markandya, Anil and Barber, Edward B. (1989) *Blueprint for a Green Economy* (London: Earthscan).

Pettit, Philip (1997) *Republicanism: A Theory of Freedom and Government* (Oxford: Clarendon Press).

Pimentel, David and Giampietro, Mario (1994) *Food, Land, Population and the US Economy* (Washington, DC: Carrying Capacity Network).

Pimentel, David and Pimentel, Marcia (eds) (1996) *Food, Energy and Society*, rev. edn. (Niwot, CO: University Press of Colorado).

Pimentel, David et al. (1999) 'Will Limits of the Earth's Resources Control Human Numbers?', *Environment, Development, and Sustainability* 1: 19–38.

Pimentel, David, Westra, Laura and Noss, Reed F. (eds) (2000) *Ecological Integrity: Integrating Environment, Conservation, and Health* (Washington, DC: Island Press).

Plumwood, Val (1993) *Feminism and the Mastery of Nature* (London: Routledge).

—— (1995) 'Nature, Self and Gender: Feminism, Environmental Philosophy and the Critique of Rationalism', in Elliott (ed.); first published in *Hypatia* 6 (1991): 10–16, 23–6.

—— (2002) *Environmental Culture: The Ecological Crisis of Reason* (London and New York: Routledge).

Polanyi, Karl (1957) *The Great Transformation: The Political and Economic Origins of Our Time* (Boston: Beacon Press).

Ponting, Clive (1991) *A Green History of the World* (London: Penguin).

—— (2000) *World History: A New Perspective* (London: Chatto & Windus).

Pounds, J. Alan and Puschendorf, Robert (2004) 'Ecology: Clouded Futures', *Nature* 427 (8 January): 107–9.

Quammen, David (1998) 'Planet of Weeds', *Harper's Magazine* (October): 57–69.

—— (1999) 'An Interview with David Quammen', *Wild Duck Review* 5 (1) (Winter): 15–21.

—— (2003) *Monster of God: The Man-Eating Predator in the Jungles of History and the Mind* (New York: W. W. Norton & Co).

RAND (2002) *Population and Environment: A Complex Relationship* (Population Matters Policy Brief RB-5045); accessible at <http://www.rand.org>.

Raphals, Lisa (1992) *Knowing Words: Wisdom and Cunning in the Classical Traditions of China and Greece* (Ithaca: Cornell University Press).

Rawls, John (1993) *Political Liberalism* (Oxford: Oxford University Press).

Rawles, Kate (1996) 'Ethical Implications of the Gaia Hypothesis', in Bunyard (ed.).

Reed, Peter (1999) 'Man Apart: An Alternative to the Self-Realization Approach', in Witoszek and Brennan (eds).

Rees, William (1992) 'Ecological Footprints and Appropriated Carrying Capacity: What Urban Economics Leaves Out', *Environment and Urbanisation* 4: 121–30.

—— (1996) 'Revisiting Carrying Capacity', *Population and Environment* 17: 195–215.

—— (2002) 'An Ecological Economics Perspective on Sustainability and Prospects for Ending Poverty', *Population and Environment* 24: 15–45.

Regan, Tom (1983) *The Case for Animal Rights* (Berkeley: University of California).

Rodman, John (1977) 'The Liberation of Nature', *Inquiry* 20: 83–145.

Rees, William (1966) 'Revisiting Carrying Capacity', *Population and Environment* 17: 195–215.

—— (2000) 'Patch Disturbance, Eco-footprints, and Biological Integrity: Revisitng the Limits to Growth (or Why Industrial Society is Inherently Unsustainable)', in David Pimentel et al. (eds).

—— (2002) 'An Ecological Economics Perspective on Sustainability and Prospects for Ending Poverty', *Population and Environment* 24: 15–45.

Rodman, John (1977) 'The Liberation of Nature?', *Inquiry* 20: 83–131.

Rolston III, Holmes (1988) *Environmental Ethics* (Philadelphia: Temple University Press).

—— (1992) 'Challenges in Environmental Ethics', in Cooper and Palmer (eds).

—— (1997) 'Nature for Real: Is Nature a Social Construct?' in Chappell (ed.).

Routley, Richard (1973) 'Is There a Need for a New, an Environmental Ethic?' (Varna: Proceedings of the 15th World Congress of Philosophy): 205–10.

Routley, Richard and Routley, Val (1979) 'Against the Inevitability of Human Chauvinism', in K. E. Goodpaster and K. M. Sayre (eds), *Ethics and Problems of the 21st Century* (Notre Dame: University of Notre Dame Press).

Rowe, Stan (1997) 'From Reductionism to Holism in Ecology and Deep Ecology', *The Ecologist* 27 (4) (July/August): 147–51.

—— (1995) 'Managing Profligacy Efficiently', *Real World* 12 (Summer): 7–9.

Rowe, Stan (2002) *Home Place: Essay on Ecology*, 2nd edn. (Edmonton: NeWest Publishers).

Ruddick, Sara (1989) *Maternal Thinking: Towards a Politics of Peace* (New York: Ballantine).

Ruskin, John (1998) *The Genius of John Ruskin: Selections from his Writings*, ed. John D. Rosenberg (Charlottesville: University of Virginia Press).

Ryder, Richard (1973) 'Victims of Science', in Stanley Godlovitch,

Rosalind Godlovich and John Harris (eds), *Animals, Men and Morals* (New York: Grove Press).

Salleh, Ariel (1984) 'Deeper Than Deep Ecology: The Ecofeminist Connection', *Environmental Ethics* 6: 339–45.

—— (1992) 'The Ecofeminism / Deep Ecology Debate: A Reply to Patriarchal Reason', *Environmental Ethics* 14: 195–215.

—— (1993) 'Class, Race, and Gender Discourse in the Ecofeminism / Deep Ecology Debate', *Environmental Ethics* 15: 225–44.

—— (1997) *Ecofeminism as Politics: Nature, Marx and the Postmodern* (London: Zed Books).

—— (2000) 'In Defence of Deep Ecology: An Ecofeminist Response to a Liberal Critique', in Katz et al. (eds).

—— (2002) 'Destabilising the Rhetoric of Production', *Tamkang Review* 32 (3–4): 95–109.

—— (2002b) Review of Warren's *Ecofeminist Philosophy* (2000) in *Environmental Ethics* 24: 325–30.

Sandel, Michael J. (1996) *Democracy's Discontent* (Cambridge, MA: The Belknap Press).

Schwartz, Peter and Randall, Doug (2004) 'An Abrupt Climate Change Scenario and its Implications for United States National Security' (Global Business Network); commissioned by the US Department of Defense; cited in *The Atlantic Monthly* (June): 50.

Scott, James C. (1998) *Seeing Like a State: How Certain Schemes to Improve the Human Condition Have Failed* (New Haven: Yale University Press).

Scruton, Roger (2001) *Kant: A Very Short Introduction* (Oxford: Oxford University Press).

Sessions, George (ed.) (1995) *Deep Ecology for the 21st Century* (Boston: Shambhala).

—— (1995b) 'Postmodernism, Environmental Justice, and the Demise of the Ecology Movement?', *Wild Duck Review* 5.

Shklar, Judith N. (1984) *Ordinary Vices* (Cambridge, MA: Belknap Press).

Singer, Peter (1977) *Animal Liberation* (London: Granada).

—— (1981) *The Expanding Circle: Ethics and Sociology* (New York: Farrar, Strauss & Giroux).

Skinner, Quentin (1998) *Liberty Before Liberalism* (Cambridge: Cambridge University Press).

Smail, J. Kenneth (1997) 'Beyond Population Stabilization: The Case for

Dramatically Reducing Global Human Numbers', *Politics and the Life Sciences* 16 (2): 183–92.

Smil, Vaclav (1993) *Global Ecology: Environmental Change and Social Flexibility* (London: Routledge).

Smith, Barbara Herrnstein (1988) *Contingencies of Value: Alternative Perspectives for Critical Theory* (Cambridge, MA: Harvard University Press).

—— (1997) *Belief and Resistance: Dynamics of Contemporary Intellectual Controversy* (Cambridge, MA: Harvard University Press).

Smith, Mark J. (1998) *Ecologism: Towards Ecological Citizenship* (Milton Keynes: Open University Press).

Smith, Mick (2001) *An Ethics of Place: Radical Ecology, Postmodernity, and Social Theory* (Albany: State University of New York Press).

Snyder, Gary (1990) *The Practice of the Wild* (San Francisco: North Point).

Solomon, M., Van Jaarsfeld, A. S., Biggs, H. C. and Knight, M. H. (2003) *Conservation Targets for Viable Species Assemblages* 12: 2435–41.

Soper, Kate (1995) *What is Nature? Culture, Politics and the Non-Human* (Oxford: Blackwell).

Spencer, Colin (1993) *The Heretic's Feast: A History of Vegetarianism* (London: Fourth Estate).

Speth, James Gustave (2004) *Red Sky at Morning: America and the Crisis of the Global Environment* (New Haven: Yale University Press).

Stanton, William (2004) *The Rapid Growth of Human Populations 1750-2000* (Brentwood: Multi-Science Publishing Co).

Stenmark, Mikhail (2001) *Scientism: Science, Ethics and Religion* (Aldershot: Ashgate).

Stevens, Val (2003) 'Does Anyone Have the Answer (to the question of what determines fertility rates)?' *The Jackdaw* (February).

Stone, Christopher (1987) *Earth and Other Ethics: The Case for Moral Pluralism* (New York: Harper and Row).

—— (1995) 'Moral Pluralism and the Course of Environmental Ethics', in Brennan (ed.).

Swanton, Christine (2004) *Virtue Ethics: A Pluralist View* (Oxford: Oxford University Press).

Sylvan, Richard and Bennett, David (1994) *The Greening of Ethics: From Human Chauvinism to Deep-Green Theory* (Cambridge: White Horse Press).

Tam, Henry (1998) *Communitarianism: A New Agenda for Politics and Citizenship* (Basingstoke: Macmillan).

Taylor, Bron (ed.) (2005) *Encyclopedia of Nature and Religion* (New York: Continuum).

Taylor, Paul (1986) *Respect for Nature* (Princeton: Princeton University Press).

Thompson E. P. (1991) *Customs in Common* (London: The Merlin Press).

Thomas, Chris D. (2004) 'Extinction Risk from Climate Change', *Nature* 427 (8 January): 145–8.

Toulmin, Stephen (1990) *Cosmopolis: The Hidden Agenda of Modernity* (Chicago: University of Chicago Press).

Trefil, James (2004) *Human Nature: A Blueprint for Managing the Earth – by People, for People* (New York: Henry Holt and Co).

Tucker, Mary Evelyn and Berthrong, John (eds) (1998) *Confucianism and Ecology: The Interrelation of Heaven, Earth, and Humans* (Cambridge, MA: Harvard University Press).

UN Population Division (2002) *World Population Prospects: The 2002 Revision* (New York: UN).

Varela, Francisco J., Thompson, Evan and Rosch, Eleanor (1991) *The Embodied Mind: Cognitive Science and Human Experience* (Cambridge, MA: MIT Press).

Vitousek, P. M., Erlich, P. R., Erlich, A. H. and Mateson, P. A. (1986) 'Human Appropriation of the Products of Photosynthesis', *BioScience* 36: 368–73.

Viveiros de Castro, Eduardo (1998) 'Cosmological Deixsis and Amerindian Perspectivism', *Journal of the Royal Anthropological Institute* 4: 469–88; repr. in Michael Lambek (ed.), *A Reader in the Anthropology of Religion* (Oxford: Blackwell, 2002).

Wackernagel, Mathis and Rees, William E. (1996) *Our Ecological Footprint: Reducing Human Impact on the Earth* (Philadelphia: New Society Publishers).

Walzer, Michael (1983) *Spheres of Justice: A Defence of Pluralism and Equality* (Oxford: Blackwell).

Warren, Karen J. (1990) 'The Power and Promise of Ecological Feminism', *Environmental Ethics* 12: 125–46.

—— (1993) 'The Power and Promise of Ecological Feminism', in Michael E. Zimmerman (ed.), *Environmental Philosophy: From Animal Rights to Radical Ecology* (Englewood Cliffs, NJ: Prentice-Hall).

—— (1994) *Ecological Feminism* (New York: Routledge).

—— (2000) *Ecofeminist Philosophy: A Western Perspective on What It Is and Why It Matters* (Lanham, MD: Rowman & Littlefield).

Weart, Spencer R. (2004) *The Discovery of Global Warming* (Cambridge, MA: Harvard University Press).

Weber, Max (1991) *From Max Weber: Essays in Sociology*, ed. H. H. Gerth and C. Wright Mills (London: Routledge).

Wensveem, Louke van (2000) *Dirty Virtues: The Emergence of Ecological Virtue Ethics* (Amherst, NY: Humanity Books).

Wenz, Peter S. (2001) *Environmental Ethics Today* (Oxford: Oxford University Press).

Weston, Anthony (1994) *Back to Earth: Tomorrow's Environmentalism* (Philadelphia: Temple University Press).

—— (2004) 'Multicentrism: A Manifesto', *Environmental Ethics* 26 (1): 25–40.

White, Lynn, Jr. (1967) 'Historical Roots of Our Ecological Crisis', *Science* 155 (10 March): 1203–7.

Wiggins, David (2000) 'Nature, Respect for Nature, and the Human Scale of Values', *Proceedings of the Aristotelian Society* XCX: 1–32.

Willey, David (2000) 'An Optimum World Population', *Medicine, Conflict and Survival* 16: 72–94.

Williams, Bernard (1993) *Ethics and the Limits of Philosophy* (London: Fontana Press).

Witoszek, Nina and Brennan, Andrew (eds) (1999) *Philosophical Dialogues: Arne Naess and the Progress of Ecophilosophy* (Lanham, MD: Rowman & Littlefield).

Wittgenstein, Ludwig (1953) *Philosophical Investigations*, 3rd edn., trans. G. E. M. Anscombe and R. Rhees (Oxford: Blackwell).

WRI (2000) *World Resources 2000–2001: People and Ecosystems: The Fraying Web of Life* (World Resources Institute). Available at <http://www.wri.org/wr2000>.

WWF (2002) *Living Planet Report* (Gland: WWF).

Youngquist, Walter (1999) 'The Post-Petroleum Paradigm and Population', *Population and Environment* 20 (4).

Zimmerman, Michael E. (ed.) (1993) *Environmental Philosophy: From Animal Rights to Radical Ecology* (Englewood Cliffs, NJ: Prentice Hall).

# Index